Hidden Truth

Hidden Truth

Young Men Navigating Lives In and Out of Juvenile Prison

Adam D. Reich

UNIVERSITY OF CALIFORNIA PRESS

Berkeley   Los Angeles   London

University of California Press, one of the most distinguished
university presses in the United States, enriches lives
around the world by advancing scholarship in the humanities,
social sciences, and natural sciences. Its activities are
supported by the UC Press Foundation and by philanthropic
contributions from individuals and institutions.
For more information, visit www.ucpress.edu.

University of California Press
Berkeley and Los Angeles, California

University of California Press, Ltd.
London, England

Library of Congress Cataloging-in-Publication Data

Reich, Adam D. (Adam Dalton), 1981–.
 Hidden truth : young men navigating lives in
and out of juvenile prison / Adam D. Reich.
      p.   cm.
 Includes bibliographical references and index.
  ISBN 978-0-520-26266-9 (cloth : alk. paper)
  ISBN 978-0-520-26267-6 (pbk. : alk. paper)
  1. Juvenile delinquency.   2. Juvenile corrections.
3. Masculinity.   I. Title.
HV9069.R435   2010
365′.42—dc22   2010004933

Manufactured in the United States of America

19   18   17   16   15   14   13   12   11   10

10   9   8   7   6   5   4   3   2   1

This book is printed on Cascades Enviro 100, a 100% post
consumer waste, recycled, de-inked fiber. FSC recycled
certified and processed chlorine free. It is acid free,
Ecologo certified, and manufactured by BioGas energy.

In Memory of Jacob Delgado

D.U.M.M.I.E. (Daring Use of My Mental Intelligence Enlightenz)

I find it funny how one person can be judged by another
    without them ever speaking
I'm pretty sure most people see me, the clothes, the hair, and
    the first thought in their mind is thug, hoodlum
How do I know this?
I know this because every time I open my mouth and say
    something intelligent, I'm looked at like I just grew a
    new head
Does it matter if I represent blue or red or how my life
    was led?
So what if my waist and the size of my pants ain't the same?
What's that gotta do wit the use of my brain?
I know a lot of young people who feel my pain
So what if I was bad and acted up in school?
Did it ever occur to you that at the time I had nothing else
    to do?
Growin' up, boredom was my worst enemy
So I took mischief and made it a friend to me
Take a look at my transcripts
Through all my suspensions, my grades never suffered
And everything I learned sits in the back of my mind
    and hovers
Waitin' to be put to a use
I laugh when people call the use of my intellect an abuse
The legal system bugs

Like they're outraged at the misuse
Yet they never take the time to come into our world
And see that we are more than thugs with some serious issues
How can you watch everyone you grew up with get put away
    for life?
Or members of your family go through heartache and strife?
Knowin' a majority of your sisters will never be a wife
Growin' up surrounded by danger and pain
Is it any wonder that some of us are considered crimi-
    nally insane?
Half the people I know were never offered any assistance
If they was, pride spoke before common sense and said
    forget this
Of all the social workers I spoke to at a young age
I can count on a hand the ones that came close to
    understanding my rage
I was young, smart and the work was no trouble
Every time there was extra credit I quickly scored double
The majority of my school life I sat and did nothin'
I'm thinkin', if this is education they must be frontin'
When I found ways to occupy myself, I ended up in the
    principal's office
With them telling me I need help
I don't know about you, but the principal wasn't my pal
And the only help he offered me was suspension with a smile
I laugh now 'cuz I find it funny
All that time they thought I was a dummy.

—Anthony, *Hidden TREWTH*, no. 1 (May 2001)

CONTENTS

ILLUSTRATIONS

PREFACE

The research on which this book is based took place between February of 2001 and July of 2006. Between February of 2001 and June of 2004, I worked as a writing teacher in the Rhode Island Training School, the state's only juvenile prison, running weekly workshops and helping to publish *Hidden TREWTH*. Between September of 2001 and September of 2002, I also worked full-time as an Americorps*VISTA volunteer at Broad Street Studio. Throughout my work at the Training School and at Broad Street Studio I recorded my observations, many of which I have used in this analysis.

My formal research began in December of 2003, when I conducted in-depth, semistructured "oral history" interviews with ten young people incarcerated at the Rhode Island Training School and six former residents of the facility. In addition, I interviewed four unit staff, two teachers, and a head administrator. I conducted these staff interviews in December of 2003 and January of 2004.

In July of 2004 I was hired by the Rhode Island Department of Children, Youth and Families as a consultant to help think through the state's proposed reformation of the juvenile corrections system. During this time I trained a team of six Brown University students to conduct interviews with Training School residents, twenty-two of which have been included in this analysis.

During the summer of 2006 I returned to Providence and interviewed another three Training School residents and two released residents. I also engaged in participant observation at the Training School and at Broad Street Studio during this time.

As is perhaps unsurprising in research of a locked facility, I faced some limitations both in selecting young people to interview and in the way these interviews were conducted. A disproportionate number of the interviewees were young men in the postsecondary unit of the facility, meaning they were older than other residents. While most of the interviews occurred out of earshot of juvenile-program workers and other residents, the environment did not feel entirely private. Every so often a juvenile-program worker would walk by and occasionally would make a comment to the interviewee. Interviews inside the facility would also sometimes get cut short.

In sum, this analysis is based on over fifty interviews with current and former residents of the Rhode Island Training School and with facility staff, teachers, and administrators; approximately three years of observation as an employee at the Training School and Broad Street Studio; and on correspondence with three young men currently incarcerated in Rhode Island's Adult Correctional Institution.

These mixed methods make the following account methodologically "messy," as one friend put it, since it combines stories of my experiences, feelings, and relationships with standard interview protocol and academic analysis. In places it reads like a memoir, while in other places it reads like more traditional sociological scholarship. At times my presence as a young, white, college-educated, slightly awkward man is front and center, while at times I recede to the background. Along the way I have had to make hard decisions about which stories to include, how deeply to explore my relationships with people I still consider friends, and how to integrate these experiences with my emerging analysis.

What follows is my best attempt to explain what I think about young men's involvement in crime and to account for how I came to think this way. My hope is that my first-person stories will help the reader understand the relationships and experiences that have shaped the more formal academic analysis at the heart of the book.

And while I take full responsibility for my failures of eloquence or accuracy, I owe an enormous debt of gratitude to many people without whom this book would never have come to fruition.

.   .   .

I would not have been able to begin the project at all were it not for the openness, generosity, and insight of the young men and women inside and out of the Rhode Island Training School who trusted me with their stories and taught me much of what is contained in these pages. Specifically, I would like to thank Anthony and Harmony for their wisdom and for their ongoing friendship. On the other end of this project, without the steadfast support and guidance of Michael Burawoy at the University of California, Berkeley, this work would have been relegated to my own bookshelf. I can't thank these young men and women, and one older man, enough.

Along the way there have been many others who have helped and informed this book. Laura Rubin and I spent countless hours thinking about our work together as we began *Hidden TREWTH* in the spring of 2001. Umberto Crenca, founder and artistic director of AS220, and a one-man Providence institution, encouraged me to take time off of school to continue my work at the Training School, and he challenged me every step of the way. I'm a stronger thinker, and stronger person, because of him, although still not nearly as strong as Bert himself (that being said, I do consistently beat him at Ping-Pong).

Arlene Chorney, Peter Slom, and the late Roosevelt Benton helped me orient myself upon entering the Training School for the first time and were important advocates for *Hidden TREWTH* and artistic freedom in general at the facility. Our first issue would have been our last without their support. John Scott, an inspiring juvenile-program worker and administrator at the facility, was also of tremendous help as this book went to press.

Ross Cheit at Brown University introduced me to the Training School, advised my undergraduate thesis, and continues to demonstrate the possibility of a life lived between scholarship and practice. Kerrissa Heffernan, who ran the Royce Fellowship Program at Brown's Swearer Center for Public Service, of which *Hidden TREWTH* was initially a part, encouraged me to think about masculinity in the Training School years before I ever did.

Eric Tucker also provided invaluable guidance as I was getting my feet wet at the facility. Edward Ahearn, Joy James, Chris Amirault, Thomas Anton, and Janet Isserlis helped me think about the Training School from a number of different disciplinary perspectives during my time at Brown. Marshall Ganz, of Harvard's Kennedy School of Government, was especially helpful in discussing with me the limits of and possibilities for community organizing among young men in and out of prison, which has helped inform the third part of this book.

Daniel Schneider, Marshall Clement, and Ellen Love all endured countless hours of discussion about my work at the Training School and helped me begin to piece my thoughts together. The multitalented Marshall Clement also did layout for the first issue of *Hidden TREWTH*, making it more professional looking than subsequent issues.

Sam Seidel, a former director of Broad Street Studio, became my research partner in the fall of 2004 as we were hired by the Rhode Island Department of Children, Youth and Families to consult on the state's impending juvenile-detention reform. Our late-night conversations at Brown's Center for Ethnic Studies have continued to reverberate. During this project, Sam and I worked with a number of then undergraduates at Brown who conducted some of the interviews included in this book, including Elizabeth Leidel, Sarah Swett, Yasmin Paula Carlos, Alexandra Gross, Paul-Emile Dorsainvil, and Andeliz Castillo. I'm grateful for their hard work as well.

Making this project an academic book, of course, was an endeavor quite different from teaching at the Training School, from the requirements of undergraduate work, or from the policy demands of state government. Since I arrived at the sociology department of the University of California, Berkeley, I have been fortunate to find a community of scholars who have taken the time to help me develop my work. In addition to Michael Burawoy, who has read and responded thoughtfully to more drafts of this manuscript than I could ever ask anyone to do again, conversations with Sandra Smith, Kim Voss, Raka Ray, and Barrie Thorne have also forwarded my thinking. Sarah Anne Minkin, Poulami Roychowdhury, and Freeden Oeur have helped me think through this project explicitly in relationship to the scholarship on masculinity, as has the newly formed Gender Workshop within the department, which kindly allowed me to present at its inaugural session.

Naomi Schneider at the University of California Press helped me take this project several steps further. I'm very thankful for her thoughtful feedback and patience with me and for the several helpful anonymous reviews she solicited. Thanks as well to Suzanne Knott, Julie Van Pelt, and the rest of the staff at the University of California Press for their hard work in putting these words to paper.

Finally, I'd like to thank Teresa Sharpe, who began as my friend and colleague at Berkeley before becoming my spouse. Teresa's combination of academic rigor and political commitment has helped me to see the ways that graduate study can be consistent with community practice. Teresa has also pushed me to see gender at work both in my scholarship and in our everyday lives. While her careful eye has been critical to this book, more recently we have both been occupied day and night with our latest project, our baby daughter Ella Reich-Sharpe.

Introduction

Playing at Masculinity

It was a cold morning in February of 2001 when I first arrived at the Rhode Island Training School, the state's only juvenile correctional facility. I was a sophomore at Brown University and had come with my friend Laura Rubin to propose starting a newspaper there. We had received the formal approval of the principal of the facility, in charge of educational programming, and of the unit manager of building five, the man in charge of supervising the postsecondary young men. Of course, the program would go nowhere without residents' support. Five young men, all hand-selected by the unit manager, gathered together in his office and listened patiently while I stammered through the outline of the proposal. After less than ten minutes of conversation and several hand slaps, we had a program. We started the following week, and the newspaper continues to this day.

Anthony wasn't at that first meeting, perhaps because he had the reputation for being one of the less cooperative residents.[1]

But a couple of weeks into the program a friend convinced him to try it out, and before long he was one of our most engaged participants and one of our most prolific writers.

The name of the paper, *Hidden TREWTH*, was definitively not my idea. One of the most artistically inclined of the young men in our first workshops had drawn out the title in graffiti style. I've never been able to determine whether he intentionally misspelled *truth*, or whether it was an accident, but once it had been misspelled there was no turning back. The group was attached to the misspelling and perhaps only grew more so when I started to plead.

"People will think you can't spell," I kept arguing as we approached our first press deadline.

"We don't care," many answered back. "This is for us, not for them." Between workshops, I tried unsuccessfully to convince Laura we should overrule the group and print it *truth*. After all, we were the editors, and we were sending it to the printer.

"People will think they're idiots," I pleaded.

"Adam, they decided on it. You can't just change it."

It was an early lesson for me in what collaboration entailed and in the relationship between the identities these young men were declaring for themselves through participation in the paper and the world to which they wrote. They wanted to be heard, but they wanted to be heard on their own terms. It was Anthony who came up with a compromise on which we could all agree: *trewth* would be an acronym. And after another lengthy debate over what *trewth* could possibly stand for, *Hidden TREWTH (Tabloid Realism Enlightening Worldz Troubled Humanity)* was born.

I have named this book *Hidden Truth* not only as an allusion to the newspaper but also because this book is animated by three related hidden truths. First, and most closely related to the intention of the newspaper, the experiences and understandings of these young men are often hidden from the larger public, a public that tends to see them as dangerous and pathological when it sees them at all. These young men putting pen to paper, publishing their perspectives and experiences, is itself a challenge to the narrow stereotypes and representations they must negotiate in their daily lives.[2]

Over the course of my work and research I have come to see two other hidden truths that complement and complicate this first one. Masculinity, I argue, is a second kind of hidden truth in that it motivates the ideas and practices of many young men involved in crime in ways that are only partially apparent to these young men themselves. Finally, I argue, young men inside and out of the Training School often offer a powerful political critique of the social world that has marginalized and ostracized them. Yet this third truth is hidden by masculinities that tend to reinforce and reproduce young men's marginalization.

Back at the Training School, after agreeing on the title of the newspaper, we had to figure out our logo. The same resident who drew the title came up with the image on which we settled. An angry-looking man, glaring at the reader, shouts, "We will be heard!" The logo is still used on the back cover of the paper (see figure 1).

The logo clashes sharply with the feel of the Training School nurtured by its administration. Upon entering the facility, one walks through the electronic gate and into the main lobby. There is no metal detector, and there are no searches. The smell

Figure 1.   Back cover, *Hidden TREWTH*, no. 1 (May 2001), by prophaetwo, Rhode Island Training School resident.

is antiseptic, the floors shining, and if the guys at the front desk know you they will let you go just about anywhere you please. Behind you, next to the front door you've just entered, you'll see a tile mosaic created by an art teacher at the school (see figure 2).

The piece is suggestive both of the image the facility hopes to project to its visitors and of the reality that lies just beneath

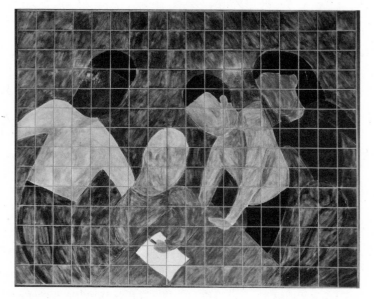

Figure 2.   Mosaic in the front hallway of the Rhode Island Training School, by Jim Anderson, Training School art teacher. Photograph by Scott Lapham.

that surface. On the colorful mosaic, a young white person sits at a table with pencil and paper, surrounded by three other young people, all of different races, and all standing. Perhaps they are all young men, or perhaps one is a young woman. The image is one of academic concentration, of collaboration, of productivity.

If the mosaic exaggerates the spirit of collaboration at the facility, it gets the sex and racial diversity almost right. Of the 123 adjudicated youth at the Training School on January 14, 2008, 110 were young men and only 13 young women. Soon after this census, the young women's unit would be shut down altogether as part of an administrative overhaul, and adjudicated young women would be contracted out to private facilities. On January 1 of the same year, 45 percent of residents at the Training School were white (Hispanic and non-Hispanic), and 33 percent were black (Hispanic and non-Hispanic); 28 percent were Hispanic.[3]

But perhaps the most accurate element of the mosaic is that all of the characters are faceless, anonymous. No juvenile is permitted to leave any lasting record of having been there, purportedly to protect individuals when, after turning eighteen, their juvenile records are sealed.[4] Most of the young people at the Training School are on the cusp of the age of majority (on January 1, 2008, about half of them were either sixteen or seventeen, with the rest evenly divided between those fifteen and younger and those eighteen and older), meaning that this was their last time getting locked up at the Training School before being sent to the Adult Correctional Institution (or ACI) down the street. Still, aside from the menacing gates around the perimeter, the Training School—upon arrival—feels more like a high school than a prison.

I was not so far out of high school myself when I left Brown at the end of my sophomore year to continue working with young men after release. Anthony was released at the beginning of September, around the time I was quite consciously not returning to classes, and we became the two newest employees of Broad Street Studio, a local arts not-for-profit organization that worked with young people inside the Training School and after their release. A week later was 9/11. That day, Anthony and I drove silently through the streets of South Providence, some of the city's poorest neighborhoods, listening to Anthony's tape of the black radical rap group Dead Prez. Occasionally, on my insistence, we'd flip to National Public Radio, where by the afternoon we would hear the beginnings of the calls for war. For all the time I had spent in the Training School, I had yet to become familiar with these streets. And it struck me viscerally that these neighborhoods were their own kind of ground zero.

Providence, like many cities in the United States, is a study in contrasts. What is home to one of the nation's leading universities is also one of the nation's poorest cities, with a quarter of its residents (and 40 percent of its children) living in poverty. Of the 139 adjudicated young people from across the state incarcerated at the Training School at the end of November of 2004, 40 were from the six contiguous neighborhoods that make up the southern part of the city. By contrast, only one was from the three neighborhoods surrounding Brown University.[5]

While the South Side was once a home for affluent owners of the city's jewelry, silverware, and textile industries, the wealthy have long since left these neighborhoods in successive waves of white flight. The manufacturing industries have largely disappeared as well and in 2000 provided only 18 percent of the city's employment (compared with 27 percent in the education, health, and social-service industries). What had been the jewelry district in downtown was recently bought by Brown to be converted into part of its life-sciences infrastructure. Most of the old factories in the South Side have met even less auspicious fates and are either empty or have been converted into condominiums for Boston commuters. But despite developers' efforts at gentrification, the median family income in the area is still around $23,000, about 20 percent of the $121,000 median family income on College Hill.[6]

The developers are part of a comprehensive program of urban renewal that has been going on in Providence for nearly twenty years, what has been billed as the city's "renaissance." One consequence has been a dearth of affordable housing, an issue Anthony and I decided we should write an article about. Anthony roped his friend Jacob into helping out. Jacob had been one of Anthony's best friends growing up and himself had just been released from the Training School. While he was still locked up, Jacob had written "Proposal for Change," a detailed recommendation for how the Training School could change its policies to support young people in getting on the right track. Anthony was holding Jacob to his words. Jacob's first assignment was to interview a local minister about the affordable-housing campaign for which the minister recently had been arrested *voluntarily*—a newsworthy story for any audience but perhaps even more compelling to these young men.

Then, as reported in the *Providence Journal* on December 19, 2001, it was over as quickly as it began: "Cutting in line at a sandwich truck didn't get Jacob Delgado any closer to a meal. But, the police said, it apparently was the reason he was killed. The police said yesterday that the 19-year-old Providence man was apparently shot during an argument after he tried to jump ahead of after-hours club-goers at one of the chimi sandwich trucks on Broad Street early Saturday morning."

Jacob's death in the early morning hours of Saturday, December 15, 2001, marked the twenty-second of twenty-three murders in the city of Providence that year. But after the protestations and exhortations from local politicians and community leaders had subsided, the death revealed itself for what it perhaps had been all along: unexceptional. A young Latino from one of the poorest neighborhoods of the city, the thirteenth of fifteen children, Jacob had been released from juvenile prison just two months before. There were rumors of gang affiliation. His death generated the standard demonstrations of outrage, and the standard sighs of resignation.

For Anthony and me, on the other hand, Jacob's death was earth-shattering. Anthony and Jacob had grown up together, had done time together. They had even been hanging out earlier on the day Jacob was killed. Anthony had suggested they spend that very evening with one another. Anthony had never lost such a close friend. I had never even come close.

I didn't hear about Jacob's death until late Saturday afternoon. Anthony called my apartment while I was out. When I caught up with him on his cell phone, he was in the midst of planning some sort of retaliation—he thought he might know the kids who had done it, and he had a friend with a van who could take him to them. Realizing that he wouldn't be telling me this if he didn't want me to talk him out of it, I was able to convince him to come over without too much difficulty.

We spent the rest of that evening together in the same manner our relationship began—in confinement. My apartment at the time was a large open loft space above a cheap clothing store in downtown Providence. A heavy and noisy grate separated the entrance from the street when the store below was closed, which it was for most of the weekend. Having let Anthony in, I kept the grate locked for the rest of the evening as Anthony oscillated between sadness and anger. I'm still not sure he realized he didn't have the option of leaving.

Instead of lashing out in retaliation, Anthony helped to organize a moving memorial service for Jacob at AS220, the local arts organization that housed Broad Street Studio. Countless former residents of juvenile prison, students, and staff from local organizations gave tribute to Jacob through songs, spoken word, and freestyle.

I look back on this series of events as both the pinnacle of my work with Anthony and the beginning of its end. Against all odds, Anthony had turned his back on the expected reaction to Jacob's death, flipping it into a moving reinforcement of his commitment to something different. He spoke of what it was like to lose a friend. But six months later Anthony would be on the run for involvement in a drive-by shooting, rumored to be retaliation for Jacob's murder. He later would be accused of robbing Broad Street Studio of several thousand dollars' worth of equipment.

We kept in touch through sporadic pay-phone calls Anthony made from Texas, until he was arrested and convicted for second-degree robbery and locked up at Rhode Island's ACI. Our correspondence then took on the unfortunately common rhythm of prison life—regular writing on Anthony's end separated by longer and longer silences on mine.

Two years after Jacob's death, I sat down with Terrence, an old friend of Anthony's and Jacob's who was still serving time in the Training School. He was one of the first young men I interviewed formally, and the metaphor he used to describe his life is one that has come to animate my own research: "I'm eighteen years old, that's eighteen years gone to the game." When I returned to look at old *Hidden TREWTH* issues, I saw the game metaphor littered throughout young men's poetry and prose. But what is the game these young men describe? Where does it come from, what are its rules, and what are its effects? Finally, why do these young men play when it seems the costs are so high? Throughout this book I explore how these young men work to achieve masculinity through their involvement in games, how these games wind up reinforcing their marginalization, and how young men sometimes find a way out.

.   .   .

When I returned to the Training School in the summer of 2006, the administration was looking for things to do with the young men in the Youth Correctional Center (YCC), the maximum-security unit of the facility. The YCC is a prison within the juvenile prison. Security is relatively casual when one comes in the main entrance of the Training School. In the YCC, by contrast, everyone has to empty their pockets of keys, cell phones, pens, and anything else that might conceivably be a threat. While many residents are allowed relatively unrestrained movement around the fenced Training School campus, YCC residents live behind a second fence and three heavy locked doors. Classrooms in the YCC all have large windows to the hallway so that the juvenile-program workers (JPWs) can keep a close watch to ensure teachers' safety. In several years of teaching workshops, the only time I ever worried about my safety was in the YCC, when one young man flashed a blade he had fashioned out of a piece of a filing cabinet.

The twenty or so residents in the YCC at any given time tend to be there for one of two reasons. Some are sent there directly from juvenile court for serious violent crimes.[7] More often, however, those in the YCC are residents who pose behavioral problems in the regular Training School units—those who have not bought into the facility's disciplinary system of points and levels. Paradoxically, then, those within the double fence of the YCC are some of those for whom the culture *outside* the Training School still holds most sway.

On my first morning class during the summer of 2006, no classroom was available for our writing workshop. Instead, we were forced to use the common area, where residents and JPWs hung out together when there was nothing better to do. The room was dark, since the light from outside filtered in only through thick wire mesh that covered a few small windows. On one side of the large room were couches, which faced a television that hung from the ceiling. On the other side, where I'd been instructed to conduct the workshop, several tables were bolted into the floor, each of which had four chairs extending from it like tentacles.

I never knew how many guys would show up for a workshop. Sometimes residents decided to sleep through them with permission from staff. Sometimes staff members locked residents in their rooms for misbehavior. And often, residents would be moved—out of the YCC to one of the less secure units, or out of the Training School altogether—without any warning to us or to the residents themselves. On my first day with this particular group, there were four residents, which made the seating arrangement awkward for the five of us. Doug was the only white resident of the group, and sat at a separate table several feet away. Over the course of the session he remained quiet, occasionally "accidentally" kicking one of the other residents at the table where the rest of us sat.

When I spoke with him alone, Doug asserted that "it's hard to be white" in this building. Out of twenty-eight residents in maximum security, only four were white. "Usually you'd think I'd get picked on," he added. But he kept it cool. While "dudes that are soft try to be hard," Doug knew that "dudes that are hard sit back and be quiet." That's what he did. And now, he asserted, he was "the only white guy in the RITS that has respect." Doug's philosophy was etched on his arm with the initials "M.P.R." tattooed in large block letters. When I asked what it stood for, he answered "money, power, respect." Allen, an African American resident also in this group, used the same acronym as he began to describe himself: "M.P.R.—money, power, respect. I get respect anyway. Say you're not selling drugs. Average nigga. Say you're making money. People start respecting you. Others see they're respecting you. So you got influence on others. If you could tell them to do something and they do it. That's power." In one way, these two young men seemed only to be making explicit the classical typologies by which people distinguish themselves from others. Sociologists have long observed that people tend to use their economic standing, their power over others, and their social esteem as markers of their positions in social hierarchies.

Yet in another way these accounts are strikingly paradoxical. Young men's participation in crime does *not* deliver "money, power, and respect" according to standard conceptions of the terms. Scholarship has demonstrated that the economic rewards of participation in the drug trade are actually less, on average, than those of a minimum-wage job (Levitt and Venkatesh 2000). In terms of power, it is hard to imagine a more powerless position than that of incarceration—a direct result of many young men's criminality. And, if anything, criminal activity undermines young men's respectability in the eyes of the broader social world. These young men strive for social distinction but seem to have defined and distributed this distinction in explicit opposition to the ways that it is understood in the wider social world.

What drives this process of distinction? Why is it important for these young men to strive for reconfigured notions of money, power, and respect? I argue that the often-unstated purpose of young men's involvement in crime is the achievement of masculinity, both individually (in relationship to one another, as they compete to be the most masculine) and collectively (in relationship to women, whom they constitute as objects). Throughout the book I demonstrate how these young men construct masculinity through a competitive struggle for distinction,[8] but I observe two radically different forms of this competition, each of which tends to reproduce young men's marginality. Furthermore, I explore the possibility that young men invested in *both* competitions are sometimes able to extract themselves from competition entirely; in the process they can reflect critically on both the practices that have previously reproduced their marginality and on the social structures in which these practices are embedded.

The high price of achieving masculinity was driven home to me in one interview in particular, one that has continued to reverberate in my mind as an echo of Jacob's death:

Interviewer: What age do you expect to live until?
Resident: Man, I don't know…like, I mean, I don't know.

Interviewer: On average, people live until they're seventy-five. What do you think?
Resident: Hmm, maybe like…eighteen. Yeah, around that.

Interviewer: You're fifteen now, right? And you think you're dead in three years. Why?

Resident: Listen, I ain't just gonna let someone come at me and not be a *man* 'bout it [emphasis added]. Like the reason I'm here is because I was tryina defend myself. Nigga out there tryina kill me, I'mna try to kill him 'fo' he gets me, but you know.... You never know.[9]

For some young men, the achievement of masculinity seems to come at the cost of life itself.

MASCULINITY AND MEANING

But what does *masculinity* mean? Sociologists have long considered gender to be a flexible but persistent social boundary, based on perceived sex differences, through which men establish power over and expropriate resources from women. But the M.P.R. for which Doug and Allen strive, while perhaps consistent with the domination of women, seem to embody a set of meanings and practices that cannot be explained purely in relationship to women. R.W. Connell, a pioneer in the field of masculinity studies, was one of the earliest to theorize the many different ways that men understand and practice masculinity. While she argues that we must continue to pay attention to "the global dominance of men over women" (Connell 1987: 183), she complicates the notion of a gender dichotomy and analyzes the multiple ways that masculinity is enacted within any given society. For her, masculinities can usefully be understood as being arranged in a hierarchy (Connell 1987, 1995), in that some ways of being masculine are "hegemonic," or more "socially central, or more associated with social power, than others" (Connell and Messerschmidt 2005: 846). While most men have some access to the "patriarchal dividend" (Connell 1995: 79; 2005) of men's general domination of women, the profits are unequally distributed.

Yet despite the intuitive appeal of this approach, the young men whom I study and with whom I worked are remarkably difficult to place within Connell's framework. This is because the term *hegemonic masculinity* seems at once to refer to that conception of masculinity practiced and perpetuated by those men with institutional power and to that conception of masculinity most *culturally* dominant (see Connell 1995: 77–78). But young men involved in crime are simultaneously some of the most institutionally powerless young men in U.S. society, *and* they serve as potent cultural symbols of masculinity. The music, fashion, video-game, entertainment, sports, and automobile industries, to name a few, splash these young men across their glossy advertisements, and the halls of high schools across the country mirror the trends these young men start. Scholars would be hard-pressed to show *either* that these men enacted hegemonic masculinity, given their subordinate economic and political positions; *or* that this kind of masculinity was subordinate to others, given its cultural prominence and power (see Sewell 1997). This is not to say that these young men are in control of the cultural representations of them. Indeed, the very purpose of *Hidden TREWTH* was for these young men to combat media misrepresentations. But images of poor young men involved in crime remain potent symbols of masculinity in United States culture.

James Messerschmidt (1986, 1993, 1997) successfully extends and clarifies Connell's framework in relationship to men's crimi-

nal practice. For starters, he takes seriously the relative autonomy of masculinity's cultural significance from men's institutional
power.[10] The way Messerschmidt understands hegemony, then,
is in terms of specific practices of social interaction that are commonly accepted as masculine across social class—in contemporary society, he argues, these involve "practices toward authority,
control, competitive individualism, independence, aggressive-
ness, and the capacity for violence" (Messerschmidt 1993: 82).
Messerschmidt goes on to argue, then, that masculinity is a
"situated accomplishment" (79). In other words, in order to
enact hegemonic masculinity, in order to feel competitive
and independent, men in different structural positions must
make use of the different resources over which they have some
control (117).

Based on this theoretical reconceptualization, Messerschmidt
understands young men's involvement in crime as an attempt
by those men without institutional power to assert their masculinity outside of institutional channels (88ff.). He explains
young men's disproportionate involvement in crime as a response
to the emasculating nature of schooling (94), since most young
people attending school are deprived the sense of control and
domination associated with masculinity. Yet those middle-class
white boys, for whom schooling is an avenue to future if not
present sources of power, tend not to be involved in types of
crime that would undermine their expected futures. Those
without even the prospect of access to institutional power in
the future are the most likely to be involved in serious crime
(104ff.).

My analysis extends Messerschmidt's framework. Messerschmidt links particular masculinities to particular structural

positions too rigidly. In more recent work (2000; 2004) he moves in a different direction, using case studies of young men and women to demonstrate the ways in which masculinity is achieved within and across different social contexts.

Yet within juvenile prison, masculinity seemed neither rigid nor flexible. It was bipolar. I observed two nearly *opposite* ways men of the same class achieve masculinity in the same social context.[11]

Rudolfo, one of my first interviewees, responded eagerly when I asked him to describe himself. I thought he would describe his values or his perception of his character. But he interpreted the question more literally: "How would I describe myself? Just the way I look....I have an afro, caramel skin color, brown eyes. I ain't going to go shoot myself up and say I'm handsome, but I don't think I'm ugly neither. I think I'm decent, and I don't have low self-esteem but my stuff is right in the middle. I don't think I'm too good for myself, I don't think I'm too good for anybody else, they can see I'm not that, I'm right, you know what I'm sayin'." His description of his physical appearance elided almost imperceptibly into his feelings of self-esteem. But things had changed since he arrived at the Training School:

> I was chillin' out there before I came to the Training School, I was chillin'. Had a few dollars, had my car. Whatever, this and that. Had what I wanted, always had a clean lineup, this and that. And when I came here it's like, I lost it. I don't have nothing. I feel like, just like, I don't want to say naked, but like, nothing, nothing in my pockets, no money, choose not to get a haircut, look all bummy and scrubby, but it's just cause I choose to, that's just it though.

In contrast to life on the street, he felt "naked" in the Training School, as if he had lost what it meant to be fully himself. Without money in his pocket, his car, his thin beard shaved just so, he "don't have nothing."

Patrick, on the other hand, seemed to have *found himself* in the Training School. Asked about the point system that regulates privileges in the school, he compared the Training School to the adult prison, or Adult Correctional Institution. "I can't think of a better way to run the place, because.... Like if this place was set up like the ACI where everybody got treated the same, there was no levels and points, then you couldn't excel, you couldn't do better. You could work yourself all you wanted but you wouldn't be able to show anybody."

The Training School helped Patrick find reason to "do better," to work harder. Over time, he had been able to earn more and more freedom and responsibility within the Training School—more unrestricted movement, better work within the facility, later bedtimes, easier access to the phone, more visitors. Those best behaved in the facility even got to visit with girlfriends. Patrick did not talk about his physical appearance in the interview at all. For him, earning points—which staff at the Training School distribute and which residents cash in for privileges—was how he could prove his self-worth to himself and others. "If you do what you gotta do and you're working hard then your points are going to be there. When I see my points every week, I get nervous every week waiting for points. Not that that's a good way to live but it shows your progress to the people it matters to and to yourself. I like the points, I think it's a good idea." Rudolfo seemed to find his self-worth in outward physical displays, Patrick in the approbation of the

Training School staff, reflected in points and privileges within the facility.

These vignettes begin to illustrate two different conceptions of masculinity that vie with one another among young men in the Training School. Rudolfo focused externally, on material displays of wealth and his own physical appearance. Patrick focused internally, on being responsible and disciplined and on winning the marginal increases in power and privilege within the rules of the Training School that accompany this obedience.

Young men at the Training School often seem to feel the pull of *both* conceptions of masculinity at once. They often spoke from juvenile prison about being at war with themselves, like in this piece by Richard titled "My Enemy":

> I get the feeling that someone is out to get me, destroy what I have become....I have found this man to be a savage and I must destroy him, he is what brought me here, he is what keeps me from successfully changing my life, he tells me to do what I never wanted to do, he is what I have become, he is me.
>
> —Richard, *Hidden TREWTH*, no. 4
> (January 2002)

Many young men understand these conflicting identities as internal, psychological. Taught by the Training School to conceive of himself as a responsible, disciplined man, Richard's investment in another conception of masculinity felt like something dangerous, outside of his full control.

Martin, finally, illustrates the way his own conception of masculinity had shifted over time in the Training School. Martin was one of the few "success stories" identified by the staff of the facility, having been released about a year before the interview without reoffending. Where he remembered once "chasin'... money, girls, [and] just tryin' to have fun," over time his conception of himself and his relationship to women had changed. He recounted with some pride his recent marriage to a young woman he barely knew:

> I only know my wife for two months before I married her. Only knew her for two months—never went on a date with her, never kissed her, never had sex with her, never took her out to McDonald's or nothing, man. We just, the Lord said, "Get married," to her, told her, "That's your husband," told me, "That's your wife." Two weeks later we got married right here in this parlor, right here in this house we got married. And nobody wanted to accept it, but the Lord said, "Get married." So we was being obedient unto God, not worryin' about no one else, not worrying about we didn't like each other or not, or what does he got to offer me, we got married and we stepped out on faith. So the Lord did that for an example to other people to when he speaks to them and says, "Get married to that person," you don't say, well, why am I feelin' like God's telling me to marry? I don't even know this chick. Why am I gonna marry her? But gotta be obedient.

Martin used to treat girls like a commodity, speaking of young women in the same sentence as he spoke of the money he was chasing. While he had since become the breadwinner for his small family, even now he felt the pull of the way he had understood himself before:

> I be lookin' at myself from the past, man, sometimes I talk to my man on the phone, he's in the ACI, and I talk to him about some of the things we used to do, and we laugh and we

joke, man, but after I get off, man, sometimes I be cryin', man, and I be like, "Damn." I be like, "Yo, that was me for real." And I'm sittin' there laughin' for a minute, man, but after that moment goes by, I be like, "Wow." My wife come in, and I change the whole atmosphere, and I'm like, "Wow. Look at all them things that I did. Look at all them things I went through, look who I was. How I used to dress, and how I used to think of myself, and how I used to talk."

It was only after his "wife comes in" that he was reminded of the new man he had become.

MASCULINITY GAMES

But if the enactment of masculinity is not an automatic response to young men's structural positions, how should we understand the link between these young men's practices and the structures in which they find themselves? Thinking of these practices as participation in two different games, in which different conceptions of masculinity are at stake, helps us tease out the way that masculinity orients young men's activity while at the same time masculinity frames (and limits) the ways they make sense of the world. Treating these practices as games also helps us think about the possibility of stepping out of game playing altogether, something I call *critical practice*.[12]

Pierre Bourdieu's account of games contains important insights for my own analysis. According to Bourdieu, humans in general tend to establish hierarchies among themselves through competition within agreed upon arenas, or "fields." People use different kinds of resources to compete in different arenas and can strategically use their high standing in one social arena (e.g., money when it comes to the economic field, or a doctorate when it comes to the cultural field) to gain in another. The metaphor Bourdieu uses most commonly to describe this process is that of the game. Players' focus when immersed in a game is less on the presuppositions of the game than on one's strategic activity relative to other players. When one is playing chess, for example, one is not consistently questioning *why* one cares about winning, how chess came to be a game in the first place, or what the rewards of winning are (of which there are likely none). One's attention is on the next move, or the series of moves necessary to win.

According to Bourdieu, then, the process by which people make sense of their lives tends not to challenge the existing order of things, since the games they enter (and the way they think about competing) merely reproduce the world as they know it. Indeed, throughout the sociological literature, the metaphor of the game chiefly has been employed to explain social reproduction (Willis 1977; Burawoy 1979). Participation in a game systematically shuts down the possibility of questioning how the game emerged or reflecting on the goals around which the game is organized. This makes the transformation of games difficult, especially from a position of investment within them. At best, then, the understandings generated through participation take the form of what Paul Willis calls "partial penetrations," or half-articulated criticisms of those games that *are not* played.

Consistent with this perspective, I observe that men's participation in games obscures that the stakes of this competition are masculinity itself. Men are aware of the competition and of the norms and rules that guide and limit their behavior. They understand, at least viscerally, the draw of playing. But they are unaware, or misrecognize, what is at stake in the games they play. For those young men involved in crime, achieving masculinity entails reproducing one's own marginality through repeated cycles of incarceration or can even involve the loss of one's life altogether. On the other hand, those young men in the Training School who become invested in the facility's regime of points and levels, and an idea of masculinity concerning their own responsibility and discipline, reproduce not criminality but a kind of blind obedience to authority. One JPW, remembering a resident's "success" in the facility, described that resident's conditioned obedience: "When we went to visit the program with this particular resident who was gonna go to the program, his mother was there and we were inside the waiting area of this particular program waiting for their staff to take the kid and his mother around. And the kid was standing there with his hands behind his back and the mother said, 'why are your hands behind your back,' and the kid didn't even realize that his hands were behind his back. You know what I mean, he was just so conditioned, he didn't even realize. He said, ''Cause that's just what we do.'"

This young man had internalized the disciplinary requirements of the Training School to such an extent that they had become second nature. Young men's blind discipline reproduces not criminality but a different kind of marginality. To the extent that masculinity seems to serve as the ultimate (if misrecognized) end of the games that men play, we might understand masculinity itself as a barrier to the pursuit of *conscious* goals of one's own making.[13]

How are we to understand the variation between the games that these young men play? Bourdieu suggests that people's very conceptions of what arenas *matter*, and therefore the games they play, depend on their objective positions in social structure. Among the young men I study, two quite different games vie for young men's attention. Young men invested in crime turn their own defiance of the law into a game and conceptualize power as something physical, worn on their bodies—what I call *outsider masculinity*. Yet the Training School introduces a new game that turns submission into sport, rewarding obedience with incremental increases in privileges and responsibilities. Young men who become invested in this game see power as something granted by those with authority, something that is reflected in the "level" they have won. I call this *insider masculinity*.

OUTSIDER MASCULINITY AND
THE GAME OF OUTLAW

Young men involved in crime have little access to institutional sources of social power. They cannot distinguish themselves as men through the arenas of work, politics, or social status. They are excluded from or, at best, offered the lowest positions in the labor market; they have little or no political power; and they are regarded as social pariahs at school and by many in society at large.

One *Hidden TREWTH* author described his participation in crime succinctly:

> …my mayhem is bringing
> me closer to death
> But I enjoy it cuz if I die
> It'll be over respect
> —G-Bo, *Hidden TREWTH*, no.
> 19 (September–October 2005)

As an adaptation to this institutional exclusion, the young men with whom I worked understand "money, power, and respect" as resources that are proven through and at stake in daily interaction. These resources are "worn" on men's bodies. Money is displayed garishly through the bling-bling of clothes, cars, and jewelry. Power is equated with physical strength, not backing down from a fight, being able to dominate a woman physically and sexually. And respect is something threatened through the smallest violations of social code. I call this *outsider* masculinity, then, for two reasons. First, and most obviously, it takes place outside the boundaries of the law. But it also takes place on the outside of men's bodies.

For young men involved in crime, participation in what I call the *Game of Outlaw* lets them escape the monotony and subservience of a regulated school life in which they have little chance of success and little control. Young men establish their masculinity through buying expensive things, through having sex with many women, through not backing down from a fight. This lets them have a sense of control over their lives, and at the same time it secures their ongoing marginalization.

Men's physical domination of women (and other men) has been central to many analyses of the relationship between masculinity and crime. Connell herself (1995: 111) argues that we can understand street crime and gang violence as "protest masculinity," or as a set of practices by which some men "mak[e] a claim to power where there are no real resources for power." Connell sees violence as central to this group's daily experience (98) as physical power becomes a substitute for institutional power. This theme is picked up in other analyses of violence as well (Hearn 1998; Tomsen 2006), which see the physical domination of women and homosexuals as strategies by which institutionally powerless men shore up their masculinity.

It is not a new observation that young men in socially marginal positions seem to respond to this marginalization by placing a premium on physical displays of force, power, and style (see Staples 1982; Majors and Billson 1992; Connell 1995). Yet when these observations are used to describe "black masculinity," as they often are, the risk is that these analyses slip into racial and gendered essentialism. This is not to say that race is unimportant in the construction of an outsider masculinity. Young men's racial identities, of course, *do* affect the choices they have in the broader social world and *do* seem to affect the extent to which they feel invested in or tied to outsider masculinity. But a game approach helps us see race (like gender) as being inscribed in social structure and meaning and not as some essential identity. As explored in this book, the white young men I interviewed seemed to understand themselves as "black" when they were involved in crime. One white young man felt he could use the term *nigga* as a term of endearment when he was involved in crime, but since he's worked to turn his life around he's come to understand the term as "racist."

A game approach also helps us overcome the risk of pathologizing young men involved in crime and instead enables us to take seriously the understandings of the social world that are associated with outsider masculinity. Participation in crime, to some extent, deprives young men of a view of the crime's place within broader social structures. Yet this same participation offers young men a whole constellation of meanings and motivations within which to make sense of their lives. Young men's understandings of the world emerge alongside, and are often inseparable from, the constraints they face and practices they take part in among others. This idea is explained by Michael Burawoy (1979: 18), who writes that "it is lived experience that produces ideology, not the other way around. Ideology is rooted in and expresses the activities out of which it emerges." Masculinity is not—by and large—imposed from the top down. Rather, it emerges in practice through the contests and contestations that make up young men's lives.

Moreover, given these young men's *lack* of investment in masculinity games played by the powerful, they have several important—if partial—insights into the social world from which they are excluded. More generally, it is the groups not invested in particular games that are most easily able to critique them. The games created by the marginalized, then, can have paradoxical effects: on the one hand, they reproduce powerlessness; on the other hand, they offer some of the most radical insight into the systems of power from which the marginalized are excluded. We see both of these qualities in the Game of Outlaw played by young men in Providence. This paradoxical quality of game playing by the marginalized—that it opens up possibilities for insight at the same time it reproduces the social world out of which it emerges—has been well captured by others (Willis 1977), if rarely linked explicitly to masculinity (for an exception, see Klubock 1996).

Paradoxically, those young men most invested in displaying their masculinity may be those men *least* invested in masculinity as an institutional boundary across which men appropriate resources from women in the market and politics.

INSIDER MASCULINITY AND
THE GAME OF LAW

We all came together and decided on what were the
behaviors that we wanted to emphasize in the school....
And basically they were focused around respect, you know,
respect for property, respect for people, respect for ladies'
language, you know.

—Training School teacher

Men who have access to institutional sources of social power
seem to stake their masculinity less on daily interaction. Instead,
the games they play are games related to their trajectories
through the workplace, political power, and social standing.
This is not to say that these games do not also involve outward
"displays" of masculinity or jockeying for position within social
interactions. But these games are more firmly rooted within
existing arrangements of economic, political, and social power
and are hegemonic, in a Gramscian sense, in that they set the
parameters for the lives of those with less power.

I call this *insider masculinity*, again as a play on the word *inside*.
Masculinity understood in this way is, most obviously, inside the
boundaries of the law. This is not to say that men with institutional power behave less violently or despicably than those
without—as histories of state violence and corporate exploitation make clear (see Sabo et al.: 13). But to the extent that these
men create and enforce the law, it makes sense to think of them
as within it. Men invested in insider masculinity also seem to
relate to power as an internal phenomenon, something that
inheres in the person rather than being expressed or worn externally. Masculinity is won less through one's daily presentation-

of-self and physical force and more through institutional position and the ongoing accumulation of resources by legal means. Men's power over women is secured through the establishment and perpetuation of these institutional inequalities, through men's paternalism and women's dependency, through state power and the labor market (Connell 1987; W. Brown 1992).

The staff and administrators of the juvenile prison, of course, suffer no illusions that they are training the next generation of economic or political leaders. But amid the contradictory and confused rhetoric and programming at the Rhode Island Training School emerges a system by which the state attempts, imperfectly, to generate consent to broader arrangements of social power. The Training School tries to do this by setting up a game, which I call the *Game of Law*, within which incarcerated young men can win small and symbolic gains in social power through consenting to the demands of those men with more authority. Those with authority are able to create arenas in which subordinate men are able to compete that do not challenge the presuppositions on which broader arrangements of social power are based.

Within the Rhode Island Training School, the rules of the Game of Law are dictated by the staff and administration. Young men win "points" for behavior in keeping with the managerial needs of the facility. These points are aggregated over the course of weeks and months into "levels," which win residents privileges such as later bedtimes and more contact with the outside world and that can be lost with any indiscretion. Yet this game would not work unless the rules and rewards put forward by the staff were not at least in part incorporated into young men's understandings and practices, unless it *mattered* to young men who got to go to bed later. Through young men's participation in the Game of Law, they practice insider masculinity, even without its associated power. They treat women chivalrously. They learn how to balance a checkbook and other "life skills." They repent for their "thinking errors," as the Training School calls them, and learn to take responsibility for themselves, not to "place blame" or to "be a victim."

The Game of Law serves two purposes simultaneously. First, it is a kind of lubricant for the daily operation of the facility. To the extent that points become the primary currency young men deal with while in the facility, Training School staff are able to maintain a great degree of control over their charges. In this way, the Game of Law resembles the shop-floor games articulated by scholars of the labor process (Haraszti 1978; Burawoy 1979). The Training School (like the firm) sets the terms of the game in such a way so as to fulfill banal organizational mandates, all the while letting players feel a sense of agency or control in their daily life. In the factory, the games workers play ensure the realization of surplus value, since workers "make out" only when the value of the goods they have produced has far exceeded their wages. In the Training School, where the maintenance of order takes precedence over any concrete output, young men are rewarded through "producing" obedience. In some ways the paradoxical nature of this game—that young men are distinguishing themselves around being the *most subservient*, or *most indistinguishable*—is even more evident in this case than it is in the factory.

Yet the Game of Law serves a second broader, if less fully articulated, purpose. Staff quite clearly view a resident's "level" as an indication of his rehabilitation, assuming that those young men who walk with their hands behind their backs on command will be able to handle the responsibilities of work and family life. In other words, the Game of Law is seen as a mechanism through which young men's marginal position within broader systems of social power can become meaningful to these young men. The Game of Law turns *submission* into sport. When successful, it makes possible a process by which young men become invested enough in conforming to the law that they consent to remaining relatively powerless within society as a whole. The points that young men collect for good behavior are acquired and saved, not cashed in. And power is understood as the power of self-control, a power that is the internalization of the Training School's disciplinary regime.

Despite its connotations of social power in relationship to women, masculinity can thus serve as a mechanism by which consent is generated among men of subordinate status. Those without social power may become invested in masculinity games, structured by those with more authority, as marginalized men compete for small and insignificant gains in power within a broader world in which they remain powerless. Young men at the Training School who play the Game of Law surrender any real control over their lives in exchange for small increases in administrative privileges. Through this mechanism, writ large, those with power are able to sustain their power, while those without "make out" with little more than a later bedtime.

Michael Messner's study (1992) of sports and masculinity is useful in its demonstration of the relationship between outsider and insider masculinity, highlighting variations by social class in the ways that young men relate to sports as they grow from the relative powerlessness of adolescence to positions of varied social standing. Sports serve as a kind of analogy to the conception of outsider masculinity elaborated above. While still within the boundaries of the law, sports offers an arena within which men's physical prowess is rewarded through strategic action within a set of rules. As an interviewee of Messner (1992: 38) observes, in some low-income communities of color young men feel "'you were either one of two things: you were in sports or you were out on the streets being a drug-addict, or breaking into places.'" For these young men, sport quite literally becomes a substitute for playing the Game of Outlaw.

Yet where men of lower social class continue to depend on sports as a marker of masculinity as they grow up, according to Messner, middle-class men tend to come "to view a sport career as 'pissing in the wind' or as 'small potatoes'" compared to their "other educational or professional goals" (135). As the possibility of hinging one's masculinity on one's more general power in society opens up, the need to prove it within the sports arena fades. This is clearest in the contrast Messner draws between Ray, a Vietnam veteran and bus driver, and Jim, a dentist. For Ray, his continued attachment to sports—despite severe injuries—lets him feel that he is "still somebody" (135). Despite his previous athletic accomplishments, on the other hand, Jim thinks, "'I'm thirty-two years old, and so what if I'm out of shape?'" (136). A similar dynamic can be observed in terms of young people's investment in crime over the course of their own life spans.

CRITICAL PRACTICE AND GETTING OUT OF THE GAME

How do we explain the *Hidden TREWTH?* Or more generally, how do we make sense of the moments at which men begin to question the social structure out of which masculinity games emerge? Several scholars have commented on the possibility of work that challenges existing configurations of gender domination—whether social reforms at the level of the state and economy, or "men's groups" within which men reflect on and commit to challenging their own violence toward women (see Cohen 1991 and Peacock 2003, both in Connell 2005). Within prisons there is a history of antisexist work among men as well (Burton-Rose 2001; Breiman and Bonner 2001; Denborough 2001). How do we make sense of these possibilities?

While Bourdieu's game playing is useful for understanding young men's criminality, and their adaptation to the rules of incarceration, his most explicit explanation for the emergence of games is a functionalist one, and therefore somewhat unsatisfying. He writes that through "investment in a game and the recognition that can come from cooperative competition with others, the social world offers humans that which they most totally lack: a justification for existing" (1997: 239).

Game playing provides a solution to the opposite (and seemingly *instinctual*) poles of the boredom of routine and the radical uncertainty of existential meaninglessness. The combination of collaboration and competition inherent in games provides players with a manageable level of uncertainty that draws them into playing. A game provides players with enough uncertainty to be interested but with enough control to feel as if their actions are related to the outcomes at stake (Burawoy 1979: 87). People are able to find a "justification for existing" through a social interaction that lets them identify their position vis-à-vis others and lets them feel that their own behavior has something to do with this position.

But a *need* for a justification for existing does not in itself produce that justification. And the particular justification for existing that the game seems to provide—a kind of individual, positional identity within a group—seems to be only one of several conceivable justifications. What about the bond one feels with another human? What about a reflective understanding of what makes one's own experience possible, a freedom from the rules of games that are not of one's own making, a freedom to posit one's own goals outside of these games? Bourdieu seems to turn everything into a game, when the metaphor seems more useful for particular patterns of social interaction than others.

In other words, we should think carefully about types of practices that are *outside* the game. In my work, those young men able to step *out* of masculinity games were those for whom a broader critique of the social world seemed to become possible.[14] When young men stop playing the Game of Outlaw or Game of Law, they step outside of the instrumentally rational, positional orientation they have had to others. Instead of thinking about power as something to be competed over individually, they begin to recognize their own collective institutional powerlessness. New possibilities are opened up for what I call *critical practice*—a capacity to come together as a group, to recognize one another as fully human (rather than as instruments), to discuss what values are most important to them, and to pursue those values together.

Young men involved in critical practice reframe money as important only in terms of meeting their natural needs and are no longer concerned with displaying or saving their money to distinguish themselves. They reimagine power as the capacity to address their problems collectively through political praxis. And respect, formerly something "won" through competition with other young men, becomes something akin to mutual recognition, or love.

Critical practice is associated with a kind of *degendering* for these young men, as they become less invested in proving their masculinity through narrow game playing. They begin to establish egalitarian relationships with the women they love, and with one another. They begin to contest their own institutional powerlessness. This is not to say that gender categories lose their salience entirely for them. But for those young men engaged in critical practice, their investment in masculinity seems to fade. At the very least, masculinity loses its rigidity, becomes one of many different identities and boundaries with which they can experiment and play.[15] Indeed, it seems, a full critique of the social world is possible for these young men only once they begin to divest from the games on which they have staked their masculinity.

For these young men, both *outsider masculinity* and *insider masculinity* come to be seen as narrow and unreflective orientations toward the social world. They begin to understand their own involvement in crime as a *part* of the social structure from which they wish to rebel, part of the same structure that offers them only marginal positions in the social world. Crime becomes "falling into the trap" of the society they see as confining at the same time low-wage work is seen as its own kind of trap.

Some young men in the Training School seem able to achieve this second-order understanding of the games they have played. This is the case, I argue, because of the contradictory identities young men are asked to assume there. The Training School intensifies the pressures of the Game of Outlaw, as young men from different neighborhoods and gangs are forced into close proximity with each other and labeled juvenile delinquents. Yet it also intensifies the pressures of the Game of Law, as staff enforce a rigid disciplinary regime on young men. Asked to play two different and opposing games in the facility, to aspire to two contradictory ideals of masculinity, some young men are able to synthesize the two through a kind of second-order reflection on each game as a game. This is a first step toward being able to step out of the games entirely and to achieving critical practice.

Some young men subsume one game within the other, either using their time in the facility to increase their status on the street or "seeing the light" and working to foster insider masculinity within themselves. Yet some, feeling the irreconcilability of these two games from a position of investment in both, develop a second-order understanding of these games and their limitations. Through the synthesis of these opposed conceptions of masculinity, young men begin to envision a world in which they can consciously create and pursue their own goals. Interestingly, this possibility seems to emerge not with a divestment from games entirely, but rather from a position of deep investment in two *contradictory* games. Where a position of noninvestment can open up a certain amount of insight into those games that are not played, a position of contradictory investments seems to create the possibility of the transcendence of games altogether.

OUTLINE OF THE BOOK

Throughout this book, as I explore the games young men play and the possibility for getting out of the game entirely, I alternate between an analysis of the structures of the games—their rules, their stakes, and the wider social world within which they emerge—and an analysis of the ways that young men (and a few young women) make sense of them, and of themselves. The first part of the book focuses on outsider masculinity. In chapter 1, I examine the rules that seem to guide all young men's participation in crime, what these young people consider the stakes to be, and how outsider masculinity represents an adaptation to institutional powerlessness. Specifically, I examine the way in which young men establish the Game of Outlaw as a realm devoid of women and the way that they conceive of, and make use of, money, power, and respect in their competitions over and enactments of masculinity.

Yet there is variation in young peoples' understandings of their participation in the Game of Outlaw—variation that I explore in chapter 2. Participants can agree on the rules and stakes of a game without having the same understanding of why they are involved. The extent to which this variation is correlated with racial differences among residents suggests the close affinity (in residents' minds) between outsider masculinity and poor men of color. Black and Latino residents tend to speak of their participation in the Game of Outlaw as an expression of "who they really are," where white residents are more likely to discuss participation as enacting a "role" or "pretending to be someone they're not." Paradoxically, those young men who most fully identify with the Game of Outlaw have some of the most sophisticated critiques of the social world that has led them to it. These young men look to criminal engagement as a surrogate for work and family and are quite articulate about the social structures that have left them without either. I call their analysis a *pure critique*, a critique that contains insight into the world but is removed from practical activity and so legitimizes their own continued participation in the Game of Outlaw.

The second part of the book focuses on insider masculinity. When young men enter the Training School, a new game is introduced, the Game of Law, with its own rules and rewards enforced by staff and administrators. I explore this game in chapter 3 and notice that the conceptions of money, power, and respect on which it is based differ radically from how the concepts are understood in the Game of Outlaw. Conflating the goals of rehabilitation and management underneath the rhetoric of personal responsibility, the Training School seeks to instill in young men the desire to be disciplined workers and husbands. Those who play the Game of Law seem to have adopted a view of the social world that I label a *pure idealism*, whether in the form of a dogmatic religious belief or a radical separation between their work lives and the realms of their lives in which they can express who they "really" are.

The young men I studied react to prison in one of three ways. I explore these differences in chapter 4. Some incorporate the juvenile prison into their understanding of the Game of Outlaw, using prison time to reinforce their conception of outsider masculinity and enhance their resources in the Game of Outlaw. Other young men accept the Game of Law at its word and try to live up to the conceptions of masculinity the juvenile prison elaborates. Each of these games uses the other game as its reference point, and each of these adaptations fails: the former through enhanced commitment to the Game of Outlaw, the latter through a "successful" escape from crime into the world of low-wage work.

The third part of the book focuses on critical practice. In chapter 5, I observe that some young men at the Training School work to reconcile the two games, the Game of Outlaw and the Game of Law, without subsuming one within the other. Paradoxically, out of the tensions between the two games, the opportunities and constraints presented by each, new possibilities emerge for reflection on and the transformation of each game. The young men reevaluate the need to use money and power as ways of competing with one another and begin to articulate a collective notion of power. Those who successfully reconcile both games have a more sophisticated political understanding of crime and their own position and seem to have the most hope for staying out of prison and engaging in political work on the outside. This convergence of the two games opens up a space of critical practice.

Chapter 6 explores the possibility of critical practice outside of juvenile prison. Focusing on AS220's Broad Street Studio, an organization that works with young people after release from the Training School, it discusses the ways in which the organization succeeds at sustaining critical practice. Young men, alongside young women, work to enact new conceptions of work and family to sustain their newfound consciousness and political work. Released into a world that has not changed since their incarceration, however, critical practice is difficult to sustain outside prison. Where the Game of Outlaw is relatively weak inside the prison, it remains strong on the outside. And where young men may continue to understand their desistance from crime as political on the outside, this understanding gets little support from an environment that provides much more resources and support to both the Game of Outlaw (drug money, peer status, etc.) and to the Game of Law (drug testing, surveillance, etc.) than it does to critical practice.

Finally, I explore the implications of the book for criminological scholarship and for juvenile correctional reform. I argue that the criminological literature is limited because it fails to acknowledge the role of masculinity in crime. I also argue that juvenile correctional reformers should consider the role criminally involved young men might play in bringing about needed reforms.

PART I

Outsider Masculinity

Home. Anthony was six years old when he got a haircut and saw, for the first time, a scar above his left ear. He asked his mom about it. She told him that his father had punched him in the head as an eleven-month old. Apparently he had been crying too loudly. Anthony learned that people who "are supposed to love you" don't necessarily follow through.

First grade. Anthony wrote his initials in finger-paint during class. He didn't think twice about writing A.S.S. until he got sent home. Despite the teacher's eventual apology, Anthony still had to serve his suspension. The experience taught him that "even if you're not doing nothing wrong you can still get fucked."

Before the age of ten, Anthony had developed a disappointment in his father and an adversarial relationship with his school. In our work together he regularly referred to his father as "the sperm donor" and to Hope High School, one of the several schools from which he'd been expelled, as "Hopeless High."

Elements of Anthony's story are remarkably common among the young men (and few young women) incarcerated at the Rhode Island Training School. On January 1, 2008, a full 47 percent of adjudicated youth at the facility had at some point been victims of documented child abuse or neglect. Almost half of Training School residents with academic records on file received special-education services, and the average test scores for reading and math skills among residents were at fifth-grade levels (with the average age of those tested 16.7).[1]

By the time he was a teenager, Anthony had learned how to steal cars and was practicing his newfound skill across Providence. While Anthony looks African American, he has Narragansett Indian in his blood, and he periodically ducked onto the local reservation to avoid the state police. Around this time Anthony adopted the tag "Wyzdom," or "Wyz" for short. With a cousin ("Diz") and a couple of close friends (also with rhyming tags), he fashioned himself a member of a set within the Folk Nation gang.

Anthony was never sent to the Training School for a violent offense. Likewise, two-thirds of the young men in the school in January of 2008 had not been arrested for violent offenses either. Of 110 adjudicated young men at the facility, 24 had been arrested for property crimes, 20 for violating their probation, and 13 for drug-related offenses. The most common violent crime was simple assault, a misdemeanor involving violence or the threat of violence without the use of a deadly weapon, for which 20 young men had been arrested. Only 7 had been arrested for felony assault and 4 for sex crimes.[2]

Anthony's first Training School bid was less than fear-inspiring. He had been drinking heavily the night before and woke up without knowing exactly where he was. It only occurred to him that he was in the detention facility when he went to get his coat and found the closet locked.

That same day, after going to court and getting sentenced, Anthony returned to the Training School to find "pretty much the whole hood" there: old friends from school, people he hadn't seen in some time. It was "more like a camp than anything else."

In Anthony's mind it wasn't a place that would make anyone think twice about getting arrested, since everyone realizes "nine out of ten of their boys are there anyway." It certainly didn't make Anthony think twice. Over the course of the next few years Anthony would be in and out of the facility several times.

Through playing the Game of Outlaw, young men enact an outsider masculinity that is outside the boundaries of the law and that defines masculinity as something displayed on the outside of men's bodies and through one's toughness in everyday interaction. This conception of masculinity makes possible a certain critique of institutional power, yet it is a limited critique, which becomes a rationalization for young men's continued criminal involvement.

CHAPTER ONE

Outsider Masculinity and the Game of Outlaw

Luis was quiet at the beginning of our interview. He used words carefully and largely kept to himself in the barracks-like unit in which groups of twenty young men live together at the Training School. Terrence was one of his few friends in the facility, and it was at Terrence's suggestion that Luis agreed to sit down with me at all. Luis was one of the more understated and deliberate young men with whom I had come into contact at the facility, and I was surprised by the way he answered me when I asked him to describe how he was before he arrived at the Training School: "Crazy. Yeah, I done a lot of stupid things that I'm not proud of today, but things that I was put in positions where I had to do them. Well, I felt I had to do them. There was probably better ways to get out of it, but I thought of it like there was only one way, and that's the way. And it was always the negative way. So I think, 'Crazy.'"

Luis described himself as "crazy," but then backtracked to say he "had to do" the crazy things he did, or at least felt he had to do them. To win the "money, power, and respect" of outsider masculinity, these young men must perform a controlled craziness, an irrationality that follows a fairly standardized set of rules and rewards.

The Game of Outlaw is what I call the set of rules, understandings, and rewards that provide a framework for the achievement of outsider masculinity. It is an agreement not to contact the police; an agreement to grant respect to those among them who are able to get money, regardless of how it has been acquired; an understanding that particular groups use particular symbols to identify themselves as members; an agreement that "turf" will be respected and that violence will result when it is not; an agreement to separate, by and large, the brutality of crime from the family lives to which young people often return at the end of the day.

This game is constituted and perpetuated by young men themselves, although it is framed by and must be understood in relation to those sources of power *not* available to them. Flashy displays of money compensate for young men's marginal economic position. The identification, acquisition, and protection of turf, the physical landscape on which the Game of Outlaw takes place, are processes that serve to reclaim and reconfigure land owned by absentee landlords and the state. Violence is an ever-present threat among participants, serving as a sanction for those who violate the rules of the game, a demonstration of power by one individual or group over another, and, collectively, as the symbolic reappropriation of political power among participants. In response to processes that deny them the social power necessary to enact insider masculinity, young men respond with an outsider masculinity that secures their ongoing marginalization.

SITUATING THE GAME OF OUTLAW

What are the conditions in which young men find themselves as they enter the Game of Outlaw, and from where have these conditions arisen? It might be useful to understand the Game of Outlaw in relationship to the movements among black Americans in the 1960s and 1970s—a moment of transition and crisis for masculinity in general, but especially for men of the inner city. Connell (1987) observes that new organizations of masculinity often take place when old forms have come into "crisis." Messner (1992), in his rich discussion of sports as an arena in which men produce and contest masculinity, examines the historical context within which competitive athletics emerged. Organized sports, he suggests, came to fruition in the United States during the transition from small farms and petty industry to large-scale urban manufacturing around the turn of the twentieth century. Men used sports as a homosocial arena in which to combat threats to traditional male roles as property owner and breadwinner, both of which felt uncertain in the emerging industrial economy. Men's physical strength and athletic prowess could freshly distinguish men from women. In a similar way, the Game of Outlaw can be understood at least in part as a response to a "crisis tendency" in masculinity for African American men over the last several decades.

This proposition, of course, implies that participation in crime is in some ways a "black" phenomenon—a collective response to the unfulfilled promises of an earlier era. Participation in most sorts of crime is coded black for the young men in this study. This is far from saying that black people commit all or most crime. Indeed, at least half of those incarcerated at the

Training School at any given time are white. But young men involved in crime, regardless of their race, seem to understand themselves as acting "black"—a phenomenon I explore in more detail in chapter 2.

In what ways does the Game of Outlaw derive from earlier political movements? During the freedom movement, black Americans formed cross-class solidarities to challenge Jim Crow segregation. The black church was perhaps the most significant organizational infrastructure for black activism during this period (Payne 1995) and further united people across classes who, living within the same neighborhoods, fought together in the cause of freedom. Alongside the church, however, two other types of organizations wielded significant power. The National Association for the Advancement of Colored People (NAACP) sought to enforce the 1954 *Brown v. Board of Education* Supreme Court decision and, more generally, advocated for black rights through the courts. Finally, groups like the Congress of Racial Equality (CORE) and the Student Nonviolent Coordinating Committee (SNCC) oriented themselves toward direct action (McAdam 1982).

It was the combination of these different forces in the movement that helped to construct the call of the freedom movement much more broadly than the legal realm alone. Indeed, the dominant metaphor of this movement was the story of Exodus, a story deeply rooted in the traditions of the black church. In this movement, then, religion was not an opiate of the masses, not the objectification and displacement of a human essence so scorned by Marx. Religious belief was itself translated into political praxis, was made part of the movement's clarion call for justice.

The freedom movement, however, became a narrower civil rights movement. Doug McAdam (1982) documents how, by the end of the 1960s, the influence of the black church and direct-action organizations had declined, while the influence of the NAACP had increased. The victories ultimately won by the movement were largely legislative, challenging the legal bases for racism in employment, housing, and voting. These legal victories opened up opportunities for a black middle class to enter the academy, to take on new professional careers, and to live among white Americans of their own class.

Yet these same victories fragmented black identity in the United States, making tenuous the interclass solidarity possible during Jim Crow. Indeed, the civil rights won by blacks during this era were consistent with an advanced stage of capitalism in which individual rights are protected at the same time notions of a collective freedom are lost. It is significant that the Game of Outlaw coalesces around the boundary of law/illegality institutionalized as a result of the 1960s black insurgency. Where race solidarity united black Americans during that period, the young men who play the Game of Outlaw find a new sort of fractured solidarity through their participation in crime.

Other movements that emerged in the 1970s, meanwhile, such as the women's movement and gay liberation movement, harnessed the energy, strategies, and legislative victories of black insurgency while hitching them to white and wealthier constituencies with more political clout (Armstrong 2002). Middle-class blacks, white women, and white homosexuals, then, were the primary beneficiaries of the black insurgency and the movements it spawned. Lower-class African Americans, who had provided so much of the impetus for the movement, were largely left by the wayside.

Scholars and journalists have documented how violent inter-gang crime decreased in Los Angeles during the period in which black political organizations were most powerful in the 1960s (Alonso 2004; Keiser 1969), a time during which aggression was focused more pointedly at political elites. Indeed, many of the most powerful and brutal street gangs today were established during the late 1960s, and understood themselves, at least initially, to be consistent with political revolution. After the civil rights movement, poor black men were left with circumstances largely unchanged.

What had changed was that the social and economic upheavals of the 1970s and 1980s had made the distinctions between poor young men and women less salient. Economically, young men were denied the dignity of a secure job, as much of manufacturing moved overseas. The dramatically declining rates of unionization over the course of the 1970s are indicative of this decline in worker power vis-à-vis their employers. Those young men who had previously enjoyed a modicum of market power found themselves jobless, while their female counterparts increasingly entered the job market in the service sector (Hochschild 2003).

Power relationships within the family were changing as well. Within families, women were contributing an increasing percentage of earnings, meaning that they had more power in relationship to the men with whom they lived. Relatedly, there was less tolerance for the intimate partner violence that represents the most brutal form of patriarchal control within the family. Marriage rates, especially among the poor, were declining significantly as well. With no economic power, and decreasing power within the family, poor young men were losing everything that symbolized masculinity in the broader social world.

In the meantime, what "integration" seemed to have wrought for the majority of poor black young men in the United States was little more than the cooptation of "hip-hop culture" by industries looking for new trends to introduce to wealthy, white high-school students. As these young men carved out a space in the social world for themselves, their music and styles became the next new thing desired by all young men.

In the pages that follow, I argue that crime constitutes the assertion of an outsider masculinity. This masculinity retains an element of critique evocative of the years of black insurgency, but it is a *pure critique*, a critique removed from political practice, which serves to legitimize the Game of Outlaw and so reproduce it.

THE CONSTRUCTION OF A SEPARATE SPHERE

For young men engaged in crime, this involvement takes place in a sphere separate from home life. It seems to represent a reappropriation of a male "public sphere" that is distinct from private, feminine domesticity. Women are in many ways explicitly barred from participation in this realm. Allen, a resident at the Training School, explained how crime is supposed to take place outside the boundaries of the home: "If you got beef with someone else, you never involve family. The Asian kid, his brother shot someone in the head. They put the address of his house, but you don't go after his mama. You don't involve family and shit. That's always been a rule. They're good rules, but I don't know who came up with them originally."

This distinction between the street and the home seems all the more significant to these young men because of the lack of male role models within the home. In other words, while some young men learn how to be men by imitating their fathers, many young men involved in crime seem to have little memory of their fathers, or have memories only of what they are committed not to repeat. Home life is then even more exaggeratedly the realm of the feminine. One writer for *Hidden TREWTH* connected his involvement in the Game of Outlaw with the absence of his father quite directly:

> And God! I still wish my Pops was with me.
> To come and get me
> Out the game.
> Now I'm the only son left to carry
> Out his name.
> —Monopoly, *Hidden TREWTH*, nos. 7/8
> (July 2002–November 2002)

A second author addressed the absence of a father more simply:

> Daddy why did you leave me?
> Is it because you wanted to be free?
> . . . .
> Why don't you want to watch your seed grow?
> And to teach me how things go!
> —Charles, *Hidden TREWTH*, no. 12
> (July 2003–January 2004)

A third writer recounted one of his earliest childhood memories of his father's abuse:

I ran out to find my father pushing my mother's back against the counter while holding her wrists. He looked up at me and yelled, "Go to your fucking room."...He walked toward me and tried shoving me in my doorway when the cops knocked on the door and opened it. He started toward the back and that's when the police were quicker.

—*Hidden TREWTH*, no. 12
(July 2003–January 2004)

Given this young man's later experience being incarcerated, his portrayal of the police—as saviors from the violence his father had been inflicting on his mother—seems especially significant. In this instance, the threat from his father was so great as to turn law enforcement into an ally.

The peer group to which many of these young men pledge, on the other hand, tends to consist of both male members of an extended family as well as male friends. Within these groups, the language of family mingles with the language of friendship. This peer group tends to replace the family at the same time it distinguishes itself from domestic life. One's "boys" can be either one's cousins or one's friends. One's "fam" can be either one's extended family or one's gang. When asked who he turns to, Paul explained, "My own people, people that I trust. My boys, my family. Friends you've known twelve years, nobody else." Only those men that he had known since the age of five, he suggested, were worthy of his trust. These few seemed equivalent to family, an extended brotherhood.

Women, with a few exceptions, are strikingly absent as players in the Game of Outlaw, a game that establishes the street as the territory of young men apart from the world of women. When they do enter the game, "girls" tend to be commodities by which young men can earn respect among other young men:

> Is there such a thing as love
> never know 'cuz I never had none
> Girls I just bagged 'em and left them alone
> give them the wrong number to the wrong phone
> —Richard, *Hidden TREWTH*, no. 9
> (November 2002–January 2003)

Women are not—by and large—those from whom young men try to win respect. This perspective is quite clearly opposed to the deep respect and love many young men have for their own mothers:

> I'm in love wit one woman, one heart man and none other than the most beautiful woman alive—my mother
> —Terrence, *Hidden TREWTH*, no. 13
> (February–April 2004)

It is as if these young men's early dependence on their mothers, absent their fathers, leads to an even deeper need to distinguish themselves from those maternal emotional bonds.

The tacit assumption of young women's passivity in the face of men's advances seeps into the accounts of staff at the Training School as well. One juvenile-program worker discussed how the social networks within which young men pursue women ensure that the next generation will be similarly disadvantaged:

> You'll get situations where kids [in the Training School] get permission and write other kids' sisters. Now kids out here, there's something wrong. Now this kid is connecting, networking with another kid and introducing him to his

sister.... So now they get out and they hook up with the girl. And they may have sex with the girl. And they may have a baby with the girl. Now we have two different kids with two makeups, which families are both lacking to some degree. Now they bring out another kid, they bring a kid into the world where the kid is gonna be lacking times two because both parents are lacking.

It is well established among young men at the Training School that they come out knowing more about crime than they knew going in. This staff member, however, extended the same sentiment to the arena of dating, as if the young women were one more resource that could be traded on the inside.

Even Terrence's espoused love for his mother became a part of his understanding of his own participation in crime, a commitment to fight to the death rather than see his mother get hurt. That this sort of protectiveness could lead to violence was driven home to me on a morning in the fall of 2001. Anthony almost never discussed his sister, Natasha. On this particular morning, however, Anthony left our staff meeting early, and I found him afterward about to catch the bus with his cousin, Edmond. Natasha's boyfriend had, apparently, been threatening her. Before I knew exactly what I was doing, I was driving Anthony and Edmond across town to Anthony's sister's boyfriend's house. Anthony and Edmond proceeded to "take care" of the boyfriend while I, naively, played basketball at the park across the street.

The paradox is that while women are in some ways treated as expendable, every woman is some man's sister, cousin, daughter, or mother. The treatment of women as expendable, then, perpetuates a different kind of assertion of masculinity, as men come to the defense of the women for whom they feel protective—on both sides dismissing the desires of the women they alternately objectify and protect.

LOYALTY AS THE BOUNDARY OF THE GAME

Loyalty is fundamental to many young men involved in crime. The conception of loyalty that emerges from interviews, however, is one that includes two distinct and somewhat paradoxical phenomena: loyalty to one's "boys" (one's group of friends or one's gang) in opposition to other young men; and loyalty to the Game of Outlaw played by all young men, in opposition to women, the family, the school, and the police. These dual loyalties provide the framework that make the Game of Outlaw possible, within which young men compete for one another's respect. Loyalty against the police constructs the field on which the game can be played; loyalty apart from the nuclear family sets up the Game of Outlaw as a substitute for the traditional sphere of male work life; and loyalty to a peer group, a brotherhood, helps define the team as well as the competition.

When asked what words he would use to describe himself, Luis responded, "Loyal. I think loyalty's a very big thing in this world, and not too many people carry that out. Um, I guess that's it, loyalty." When I followed up by asking what the word "meant to him," he pulled up his shirtsleeve to reveal a tattoo with the words "death before dishonor." He continued, "What it means to me? Like, I got this tattoo, I got it ... Death before dishonor. I got that cause it means a lot to me." For Luis, honor and loyalty seemed synonymous—that is, loyalty itself seemed a mark of honor.

As Luis proceeded to explain the importance of loyalty in his life, however, two details emerged. First, it became clear that

Luis valued loyalty highly in part because of its absence in Luis's own life. While emphasizing that his mom raised him and his six brothers "the good way," Luis went on to blame his latest stint in juvenile prison on his brother's betrayal:

> And I got a brother, that, we was partners, and because of him I'm in here now, I say. Cause we was doin', we was sellin' lot of drugs together. We was doing real good on the streets. And I got locked up for two weeks at the ACI cause I'm drivin' and they found a rock and they confiscated fourteen hundred dollars off me. Um, and I was drivin', and I did two weeks for that, I got out, and when I came out I had like six, like eighty something grams.... He said that someone robbed him, and not even four hours of me getting bailed out and I'm drivin' in a stolen car with two guns lookin' for the dudes that robbed him and we didn't find nobody. Like two weeks after that, I'm askin' around, what happened to my brother? Everybody said they jumped him, but nobody robbed him for anything. So I don't know what he did with all the money and the drugs. He got me.

Luis implied that his own brother betrayed him. It is this betrayal that highlighted for Luis the importance of loyalty: "And that's what loyalty means to me. Cause I trusted him, you know what I'm sayin', I don't trust that many people in this world, and him, he was my partner, I trusted him. He did me dirty, so I look at loyalty, like if someone's never has did you wrong, why you gonna bite the hand that feeds you?" For Luis, "what loyalty means" was exactly what his own brother did not show him. Luis did not seem to value loyalty because it was reciprocated by most of his peers, as it was not.

Secondly, it became clear that Luis conceived of loyalty at least in part as a loyalty against the police. Luis observed:

Like some people will go out there, they'll catch a charge,
and they'll just start talking just to get their sentence
reduced. And my first charge was the gun, the gun charge,
they was tryin' to give me five years. And they either
wanted me to rat or take the five years, and I wasn't rattin'.
I was sittin' in front of the judge, I remember, I was cryin'
cause he was telling me to rat or five years. I was thinking,
"Wow, I'm gonna get put away." And all he wanted was to
know whose gun it was. Who I buy it from. But I wasn't
down to say it. And I'm sure these other kids would have
just ran their mouth. That's what loyalty means to me.

The loyalty Luis described is a loyalty to a gun dealer in
opposition to a judge asking him to "rat." This was not the
loyalty of one gang or group of friends against another but a
loyalty against the forces of "law." This version of loyalty was
supported by Rudolfo, another Latino at the Training School,
who noted when asked about his experiences in the Training
School, "But as for doing time in this place it's like just whatever,
I'd rather not do time, but I ain't going to snitch on nobody
neither." Asked explicitly about the rules that guide him on the
outside, Allen answered similarly, "Never, snitch, never ever. My
folks told me that [when I was] little little. Everybody in my
neighborhood basically. Some people looking at hard times, they
didn't tell....If you in trouble, why would you send someone
else to prison?"

This commitment against turning to the police was wide-
spread in interviews:

Interviewer: If someone stole something from you or your house,
what would you do?
Resident: Not sure.

Interviewer: If someone were stealing from you, who would you tell?
Resident: Probably one of my boys.

Interviewer: If someone stole something from your house, what would you do?
Resident: I can't have them harming my family but like if they just took something, I'd try to get it back.

Interviewer: Would you call the cops?
Resident: No, I don't think that's necessary. I would figure it out on my own.

The reason why I don't call the cops is because they don't really care either. Cops are there to protect, serve, and...I forget the other thing. I know there's three things they have to do: protect, serve, and something else. The only thing they doing is making you serve time and they're not protecting you. Say I call the cops for...'cause when I got in a fight with some kid, somebody else hit me over the head with a bat, the cops came. They did the report and that was it. I never heard back from them. They were supposed to find out who it was. Do an investigation and all that. They didn't do none of that. All they did was take the report and then...that's it.

The importance of the rule against snitching was made even more apparent by the suggestion of its violation:

Interviewer: If someone stole something from you or your house, what would you do?
Resident: It depends on what they took. There'd probably be a problem. If I knew who did it I'd probably try and go and get it back. But if somebody broke into my house, I really don't want to say this but I think I'd call the cops.

Interviewer: Why don't you want to say that?
Resident: I guess it's the whole mentality. Even coming in here and you do what you gotta do you still pick up the mentality of the place and I guess that'd be considered snitching. That's not something you want to be around here is a snitch.

In late 2005, a clothing company based in Boston came out with a line of t-shirts with the words "Stop Snitching" printed in bold letters on a picture of a stop sign. The instant popularity of the shirts in Boston and cities across the country caused intense concern among law enforcement personnel, as the unwritten code of the game was—finally—made explicit (Associated Press, January 6, 2006).

Edmond, a young African American man in maximum security, went even further, answering a question about what is responsible for the violence in his neighborhood by saying, "Snitches—people that let things happen. People snitch, they get hurt, then somebody snitches about person who gets hurt. It's a whole snitchfest." It is violators of the code of loyalty, Edmond suggested, who are most responsible for the cycle of violence, not the perpetrators of the violence itself. One *Hidden TREWTH* writer wrote with similar sentiments,

> If all the snitches sew up their lips
> And had no way of communication
> Then lock up wouldn't exist
> —Avalanche, *Hidden TREWTH*, no. 9
> (November 2002–January 2003)

In this writer's mind, snitches—not offenders, nor police—were responsible for the existence of the juvenile prison.

Why might loyalty to young people not in one's immediate peer group, in opposition to the police, be important even in the absence of others' loyalty? To the extent that loyalty (not snitching) is truly a source of honor, as Luis asserted, then this might explain why young people stress its importance even when it is not reciprocated. That is, if a reputation for not snitching gives a young person status among his peers, this might be a reason to stay silent even in the face of others' betrayal.

But we might also wonder whether loyalty to the game is important to young men's self-conceptions. That is, in the sense that one's own identity or sense of self is tied to the Game of Outlaw, the illusion of a "code of loyalty" even in its absence might be an important illusion to give meaning to one's everyday activities. This sort of broad loyalty to the game—a commitment not to snitch even against one's enemies—is a solidarity that sets the boundaries or framework necessary for the game to take place at all.

Yet "resistance" by refusing to snitch is a limited and in many ways self-destructive perversion of political consciousness. Resisting the power of the police by refusing to snitch isolates young men from the public at large and from young people's own neighbors, who—even when themselves distrustful of the police—feel endangered by young people's behavior. This is not the provocation of police so strategically effective in Montgomery and throughout the South in the 1960s—nonviolent demonstration planned quite explicitly to reveal the brutality of white racism (McAdam 1992). Young men involved in criminal behavior have almost no moral authority with others outside of their immediate context.

Of course, this second-order loyalty—loyalty as a commitment not to snitch—frames a game within which young men are fractured, divided into competing teams, and the stakes are often those of life and death. Having asked Rudolfo to tell me about the "turning points" in his life, I followed up with my standard question, "Is this the story you always tell?" Yet since I had seen Rudolfo bantering with Terrence earlier in the day, I adjusted the question slightly: "If you were talking to Terrence about your life how would it be different from talking to me?" Rudolfo responded:

> I won't say me and Terrence, we not from the same set, from the same hood, but we might relate to certain things, you know what I'm sayin', like the way we was growing up to things that me and you probably wouldn't relate cause I really don't know you, I heard him say a few things I heard him talk before, we probably could relate to certain stuff that me and you couldn't relate cause I really don't know you much enough to talk to you or heard you talk about the way you grew up, this and that. So we'll probably relate just for the fact that I heard him talk, just things like, "Yeah, that happened to me when I was younger." Or just things like that.

What struck me was Rudolfo's emphasis on the *difference* between him and Terrence before acknowledging what united them. Rudolfo seemed to highlight both the potential for young people's solidarity with one another—given the similarities in "the way [they were] growing up"—and the way that this solidarity was systematically undermined by an emphasis on the differences in "set" or "hood" between young people of the same race and class background living in the same small city.

The physical landscape on which these young men play the Game of Outlaw consists of the streets in a few neighborhoods in Providence (see the introduction). Many residents from other parts of the state were in these neighborhoods when arrested. These neighborhoods form the basis for group rivalries, despite the fact that many young people will have lived in several different neighborhoods as they have grown up. And despite the physical proximity of the neighborhoods in which the Game of Outlaw is played, and similar race, ethnic, and class makeup of those living within them, young people involved in crime tend to emphasize their allegiance to one part of town at the exclusion of others. One interviewed resident noted the arbitrariness of these boundaries:

Interviewer: What do you think the biggest problem is in your neighborhood?
Resident: Probably say like gang violence and sides. Like East, South, West.

Interviewer: Why are those problems do you think?
Resident: 'Cause I'm not sure.... Like we're all from Providence. We shouldn't even be fighting with each other.

Interviewer: Do you think that can be solved?
Resident: No.

Interviewer: Do you think it can be made better?
Resident: Not really. 'Cause it goes a while back.

For this resident, the geographical divisions have simply always been there.

But what purpose do these allegiances serve? Most directly, these divisions demarcate the turf within which drug economies may operate. But these boundaries are salient even for those young people not involved in the drug economy. It seems that the battles over turf give young men a sense of property ownership or belonging in spaces largely owned by absent landlords and that this sense of ownership or belonging is as much the cause of these boundaries' existence as a result of it.

If loyalty against the police helps establish a degree of autonomy for the game, separates the rules of the street from the rule of law, loyalty to particular groups within the Game of Outlaw sets up a competition within which young people are able to vie for status and material wealth.

Young men repeatedly emphasized the importance of their peers to the meaning that they give to their lives and, more practically, to the decisions that they make and actions they take. This degree of social capital calls into question theories of "social isolation" that emphasize the lack of social networks in low-income neighborhoods. While young men may not have extensive social networks outside of the neighborhoods in which they live, they have quite strong ties to one another. These ties suggest the possibility of collective work at the same time that the divisive nature of these ties undermines this possibility.

MONEY AND COMPETITIVE CONSUMPTION

Doug explained the relationship between money, power, and respect: "Most important is to get that money. Money's everything. Money you can do whatever you want. Power over people. All you got to do is make one call. Make people do what you want them to do. Get people to respect you." He began by emphasizing the importance of money, but then went on to suggest that money was actually only a way to have power over people, which he equated with respect. An essay in *Hidden TREWTH* made a similar point:

> A flock of birds is like friends. You got bread to give
> them they stay and eat. But when the bread's gone they're
> gonna leave.
>
> —Logic, "Bird Theory," *Hidden TREWTH*,
> nos. 7/8 (July 2002–November 2002)

Respect, from both other young men and also young women, can be gained through the acquisition of money and power and seems to be the chief end of young men's activity.

Of course, the way young men go about winning respect comes with a high price. Individuals rendered powerless by the structures within which they live try to reclaim power individually at the expense of one another. This understanding of power obscures the vast power differences between *all* of these young men and other social groups and precludes the kind of organization among these young men that would let them, as a group, contest these broader power arrangements.

Money and power are the currencies with which respect can be "bought." As Terrence observed, very little of the competition that took place in the game was over resources necessary for survival: "The drug game, I seen the drug game take lives of people, my family, whatever, but nobody's hustlin' for necessity no more, nobody's breakin' the law for necessity, nobody's doin' anything out of necessity…it's all out of material. Everybody want to get out there, they want to be flashy, they want to be fly."

Traditionally, scholars of youth delinquency have suggested there is something particular about lower-class young men that leads them to value material possessions while eschewing the middle-class norms that dictate the legal means to get them. This argument, however, assumes that engaging in crime is actually profitable, an assumption called into question by research highlighting the economic activities of street gangs. A study by Steven Levitt and Sudhier Alladi Venkatesh (2000) illustrates how gang drug dealing is not especially lucrative even for those gangs organized specifically around entrepreneurial endeavors. The authors conclude: "Taken as a whole, our results suggest that even in this financially sophisticated 'corporate' gang, it is difficult (but not impossible) to reconcile the behavior of the gang members with an optimizing economic model without assuming nonstandard preferences or bringing in social/nonpecuniary benefits of gang participation" (787).

I would suggest a more complicated relationship between young men's behavior and the economic opportunities available to them. That is, rampant materialism may be as much a response (if an unconscious one) to exclusion from low-paying work as it is the cause of young people's rational decision not to engage in this work. The fantasy world of fancy cars and bling-bling is worth striving for only in the absence of real alternatives. *Striving* for material gain becomes a source of meaning for young people even in the absence of material success and can provide the prospect of glamour even in its absence. One might lose one's life, but even this potential loss of life is integrated into the understandings of the young men that participate in crime, reconfiguring the risk as a part of the drama and appeal of outsider masculinity. The ambivalent attitude with which many young men seem to relate to the Game of Outlaw is captured by a poem entitled "Ghetto," which highlights both the brutality and the attraction of participation in crime:

> Born in the ghetto
> where guns get beef settled
> . . . .
> the ghetto's the devil
> . . . .
> But then again the ghetto is a dream come true
> a place where you
> can walk around makin' loot
> . . . .
> every day's a struggle
> But ghetto I love you
> you raised me as a kid
> You're one of the reasons why I'm so wild
> plus street smart
> . . . .
> I guess this is just a love/hate relationship.
> —Logic, "Ghetto," *Hidden TREWTH*, no. 9
> (November 2002–January 2003)

At first, the author suggests that the risk of getting killed is the price he pays for the possibility of material wealth. Yet he comes back at the end of the poem to say that he "loves" the ghetto because it "raised him" and taught him to be "wild" and "street smart." His involvement in crime, and its dangers, are understood both as a "struggle" and as an important—and in some ways idealized—part of who he has become.

Describing his experience in the Training School, Rudolfo declared that it had been "just time wasted of your life, even six months, a year, whatever you got, three months, it's still time you could have done a lot of stuff out there, on the set." The "set," then, creates the metaphorical stage on which young people give their lives meaning and their time value—and so makes real the opportunity costs of time spent locked away. This contrasts with the perception of many employers, school administrators, and police officers, who see these young men as social detritus, surplus labor not even worth training for a job (Wacquant 2001).

The way one earns respect with one's money, however, is not only by showing it off but also by providing for loved ones. In this way, outsider masculinity is a way for young men to reclaim a kind of paternalism that their marginalization has made impossible. Terrence described his early participation in the Game of Outlaw: "I was out there, had my girl with me, this was in the, I was in the first, between the first grade and the third grade, around there. Had my girl with me, so I'm goin' stealin' jewelry for old girl, 'cause that's what I'm seein', I'm seein' around the hood everybody you got a girl you take care of her, I'm trying to take care of her but I ain't got no money."

Terrence began committing crime to "take care of his girl," as he had "seen around the hood." But young men do not only use commodities to provide for the women they are dating. A young writer named Ant R. described one of his best memories, which involved spending money on a young boy in his neighborhood named Sun-daddy, to whom he was not related at all:

> We went to every store we could think of. The night was basically over and we had spent $425.00 on Sun-daddy. He was gonna be so happy, that just made me happy. The next day we went to Sun-daddy's house and it was christmas. We knocked on the door and Sun-daddy came to the door. We

said merry christmas and then he let us in. He had a play
station 2, four pairs of sneakers, 6 outfits, a gold chain, and
a bike. He gave us a hug and said thank-you. His mother
gave us a hug too and started cryin. Since then his mother
has respected us like crazy.

—Ant R, *Hidden TREWTH*, no. 15
(September 2004–January 2005)

This kind of charity is the softer side of the same process
through which money offers a way of earning respect. Outsider
masculinity helps some young men reassert patriarchal norms
of the male as breadwinner and provider in a social and
economic environment in which this model has become increasingly unrealistic.

COERCIVE POWER

Money is not the only way of gaining power and respect,
however. One's capacity to inflict physical harm is also a currency of sorts. At one point, this capacity may have been correlated with a certain physical strength and agility, since young
men would fight with fists or knives (Canada 1995). With the
modern availability of firearms, however, physical agility is less
important than a willingness to inflict harm and to be harmed.
Anthony recognized the premium on craziness in the Game
of Outlaw:

Them people who got a Calico, it's a hundred-shot gun,
holds a hundred shots, sprays probably about six every time
you pull the trigger, but can't aim for shit. Motherfuckers
weigh a hundred and ten pounds, can barely control the
gun they have, but have no problem driving by someone

and emptying the whole hundred-shot clip at a corner when they only want to hit one person. And whether they hit that one person or not, their credibility and their respect in the streets goes up because they went and shot at that corner, which doesn't really make sense to me.

One's irrational use of violence can actually enhance one's credibility in the Game of Outlaw, decreasing the extent to which others might take advantage.

But violence is not only about respect. Pragmatically, violence is a mechanism to enforce contracts when other mechanisms are unavailable. If the state, as Weber suggests, consolidates political power through the appropriation of the means of violence, young men's use of violence to settle accounts might be seen as a perverted reassertion of political power consistent with loyalty against the police. Violence or the threat of violence is prevalent in young men's accounts of the Game of Outlaw, as Terrence remembered: "Then, this is where my first assault charge came from, this cat he owed me some money and I had a razor blade on me cause I kept a razor in the mouth at all times... whatever. So I cut him. I mean, I wish I didn't do it, he still never paid me. But, I mean, I look back, that's childish, that's childish, acting out of ignorance. Tryin' to take that, take that street and personify that."

Terrence simultaneously recognized how violence was "acting out of ignorance" and how he used violence in an attempt to get money someone owed him. Even Anthony, while dismissing the random violence of the streets, discussed his own willingness to use violence as vengeance: "But say someone, I don't know, did something to one of my children or someone in my family. Just because I've lost friends to violence doesn't mean I'd be any more averse to hurting that person. It might make me think more whether I want to drive by and shoot at the whole area, as opposed to catching him by himself, but I don't think it'd really stop me too much from hurtin' him if I really wanted to." The use of violence might be seen, then, as both a strategic mechanism for settling accounts and as an expressive mechanism for winning respect and reappropriating a kind of political power.

Yet the rules of the Game of Outlaw—in which violence increases young men's status and serves as a mechanism for enforcing contracts—occlude how criminal violence distracts young people from more political targets. Frantz Fanon (1963), in his account of the Algerian revolution, describes this intraclass violence as a psychological displacement of aggression against the powerful, a way of feeling power in the face of powerlessness while ignoring the real sources of oppression: "While the settler or the policeman has the right the livelong day to strike the native, to insult him and to make him crawl to them, you will see the native reaching for his knife at the slightest hostile or aggressive glance cast on him by another native....It is as if plunging into a fraternal bloodbath allowed them to ignore the obstacle" (54).

Fanon's account perhaps misses the paradox that for young men violence also represents a reappropriation of certain kinds of power: political power, as violence is used to enforce the rules of the Game of Outlaw in the place of a reliance on the police; and expressive power, as violence represents a reassertion of a precarious masculinity that wins respect among young men's peers.

OUTSIDER MASCULINITY AND
PENAL SANCTION

Surprisingly, young men and staff at the Rhode Island Training School were in agreement about one criterion that constitutes "success" in young men's relationship to the facility: not coming back. Asked what "success" meant in the eyes of the Training School, Rudolfo responded:

Rudolfo: Know what I'm sayin', never coming back, that's probably the biggest success of the Training School.

Adam: What is success in your eyes?
Rudolfo: It's not coming back, you know what I'm sayin'?... Success is just leaving this place, not coming back, and not trying to see the back of a cop car and being arrested, that's what I call success.

It is tempting to assume that Rudolfo had accepted for himself the goal of desistance from crime. In his next sentence, however, he expanded on this idea: "And having what I want, that right there is success...I just want money and a nice car, know what I'm sayin', I want to be living decent like, want to make sure my family's doing nice as long as I am, as well as I am."

Success meant both staying out of the Training School and having "money and a nice car." Success and failure are understood in strategic rather than moral terms. Success means engaging in crime without getting caught. Throughout the interview, Rudolfo made assertions like "I got caught, just by my stupidity," or "Damn if only I would have been smarter." Rudolfo did not conceive of his criminal activity as stupid. Rather, the carelessness that led to his capture was evidence of stupidity.

This strategic orientation toward prison among young men might be understood as the flip side of a juvenile justice system that has increasingly abandoned any pretense of treatment *or* punishment, where the impersonal and actuarial management of a criminal population takes precedence over moral and personal responses to criminals, whether rehabilitative or punitive (Feeley and Simon 1992). To the extent that the criminal justice system is emptied of moral content, replaced by surveillance mechanisms and "risk assessments," the Game of Outlaw is experienced even more literally as a game in which the goal is to profit as much as possible without getting caught.

Moreover, defining success as staying out of prison while continuing to engage in criminal activity implies the possibility of playing the Game of Outlaw without being caught, implies contingency in the relationship between criminal practice and criminal justice. For an outside observer, the relationship between juvenile crime and incarceration is obvious. Perhaps a young man will be able to get away with drug dealing for a month or two, but eventually he will get caught. For young men themselves, however, crime and incarceration are two separate phenomena, and the first leads to the second only through failure in playing the Game of Outlaw well.

Equating periods of incarceration with failure *with respect to the Game of Outlaw* lets young men reconcile their own choice to be involved in criminal activity with an espoused repugnance for the criminal justice system. Rudolfo was only one of many young men to observe an inconsistency between his espoused desires and his subsequent actions: "Well, to be honest with you, one thing I usually say is I didn't want to come back, even though

I had three years of probation. It really didn't change me though, 'cause I still did the same thing."

One interpretation or reconciliation of this contradiction between desire and action is that young men "like" the Training School and choose to return, an interpretation that finds some support both among young people and among staff. Choosing to come to the facility, however, is seen as pathetic and immature among young men incarcerated. Rudolfo answered a question about who "belongs" in the Training School as follows: "Who do I think belongs here? Little kids, well not little kids, but just kids that are bad asses and just keep messing up, messing up. They'll steal a car one week, and then get out, and then the next week they're out stealing a car and they're back in here. They just leave and come back, leave and come back over petty shit. You could avoid it but you just don't."

There are kids, Rudolfo noted, who "could avoid it but just don't," and those kids "deserve" incarceration. Rudolfo, of course, did not identify himself as one of these young men. Separating involvement in crime from incarceration lets young people preserve a sense of agency ("I choose to be involved in crime"), without acknowledging that they are therefore "choosing" to be incarcerated. Terrence went further, suggesting in economic terms how an occasional slipup is still profitable: "The way I see it is, there's a lot of stuff I did out there that I didn't even get caught for, and that's how people think, that's how the game works, everybody think, 'I didn't get caught for this, I didn't get caught for that. If I get caught for this little charge I still got much more dirt,' know what I'm sayin', that's why people out there grimin'."

If punishment is understood to be proportionate to the crime for which a person has been caught, and a young man is caught for only a small proportion of the crime in which he has been engaged, then this economic rationalization for continued involvement in crime makes a good degree of sense. If the law provides punishments commensurate with those activities being punished—a taken-for-granted understanding of the criminal justice system, if ludicrous upon closer examination—then one's criminal "profits" are those crimes that go unpunished. By this logic, criminal behavior is often profitable, in that one rarely receives punishment for all of the illegal activity in which one has engaged.

Of course, even "punishment" has the potential to enhance one's status in the Game of Outlaw, since surviving incarceration is seen as evidence of toughness valued by young people on the outside. The Training School's ability to enhance young people's status in this way, however, is contingent upon the premise that it is something brutal enough to be avoided. The status-enhancing quality of incarceration, then, depends on the denial of the regularity with which young men get incarcerated.

This status enhancement is supported by the literature on labeling, which suggests that the label of "deviant" can actually increase investment in criminality and status among criminals.[1] The labeling that takes place in a juvenile facility is more complicated, however, for what it symbolizes is ambiguous. Asked how he thought the Training School wanted him to see himself, Rudolfo responded: "To see yourself like you're locked up! Like, 'Look, you want to do a crime now you're doing time for it.' Even if it's here, people say oh, this is kiddy-camp, or just camp, but you're still locked up, you ain't with your family."

On the one hand, the Training School helps young people understand themselves as criminal—enhancing their status among other young people involved in crime, further marginalizing them in relationship to school and other social networks. On the other hand, young people in juvenile prison recognize that, within the criminal game itself, juvenile prison is still the little league, the "kiddy-camp." By the standards of society at large, a young man is considered a delinquent, but by the standards of "toughness" internal to the residents of the criminal justice system a juvenile offender is still a boy.

INVESTMENT IN OUTSIDER MASCULINITY AS DIVESTMENT FROM INSIDER MASCULINITY

Explored in more detail in the chapters to follow, the rules and rewards of the Game of Outlaw contradict the rules and rewards of the Game of Law. Young men who strive for standing in the Game of Outlaw are simultaneously undermining the possibility of their success in other arenas. This was well illustrated by the following poem:

What Is

What is a gang color and respect
The right to hold the tec and protect your neck

. . . .

What is school, being called a tool
Cuz you can't spell arithmetic and follow the rules
—Logic, *Hidden TREWTH*, nos. 7/8
(July 2002–November 2002)

Where involvement in crime lets a young man feel "respect" and gives a young man the right to "protect" himself, school increasingly comes to be regarded as an arena in which one is only "called a tool" since one "can't spell."

This process is legally inscribed through a young man's juvenile record, which at once enhances a young man's status in the Game of Outlaw and further decreases his status at school. At the same time Anthony was earning respect on the streets of Providence, he was getting expelled from more and more high schools. Indeed, even without accounting for a juvenile sentence's stigma, getting sent to the Training School interrupts the school year, making it very difficult for young men to graduate from high school.

A criminal record makes alternative life choices less accessible, as Terrence described: "If you sit down with half the drug dealers man, and you talk to them, 'cus, they drop some knowledge on you, they be like, 'Yo, I do this, but I feel I have no choice.' After you get a drug charge on your adult record, they feel they can't do nothing else. It's like either sell drugs or try to hustle for this Motel 6 job that's not payin' nothing, they got kids to feed."

Probation also ensures many young adults return to prison, even if they have largely stayed out of crime. Rhode Island law states that probationers can be charged with violating their probation (and get sent back to jail) with a much lower burden of proof than needed to convict someone "beyond a reasonable doubt":[2]

Adam: What are barriers you've confronted to staying out of the Training School or [Adult Correctional Institution]?

Anthony: Cops. Like in this state, once you're on probation, you're pretty much fucked. Not so much juveniles, because there's a little more leeway, but a lot of juveniles don't know the law so well, so they get caught up anyway. But on the adult side of things, any arrest, whether it was wrongful or not, any arrest is not keeping the peace, that's a violation of your probation. You can get arrested for a charge, beat the charge, and still get time on your violation. Like they determine your violation standing within ten days of your arrest, before your charge even gets to a fucking pretrial.

Even a juvenile record, which is expunged after a young person turns eighteen, sets young men up for a difficult struggle into the Game of Law. This is reinforced by the school system that actively avoids the return of young offenders, as recounted by an administrator at the Training School: "The schools generally remember the kids the way they were when they left, and so they're not anxious to receive them with open arms. And they're not particularly welcome. They are young people who have caused trouble in the schools, a lot of them, and have sold drugs around the schools and taken drugs and so forth. So school administrations generally, and/or teachers don't necessarily want them part of their system. And when you don't feel like you're wanted, you tend not to stay very long."

Perhaps as significant as the legal and scholastic barriers presented by participation in crime, however, are the feelings of investment young people develop toward their own participation. This appeared in young men's understanding of their "smarts":

Interviewer: Are you smart?
Resident: No. Well, yeah…I think I'm street smart, not really booksmart…but I don't know, maybe I could be, never really tried you know. Here I feel smart because school is a joke. I get straight As here…but I doubt that means anything.

Interviewer: Are you smart?
Resident: Nope.

Interviewer: How do you know?
Resident: Just do. Don't take no genius to know you ain't smart.…Shit, I been to school. Like some kids, you know, teachers always be telling them, "Ooh, good job, yada yada, you so smart." Ain't nobody ever tell me that in my life 'cept for my mom. You know, like street smarts I guess, but I ain't never been good in school or no book smarts, no, nothing like that.

To the extent one perceives oneself as street smart, and lacking in other forms of intelligence, continued participation in crime makes sense. One has earned the respect one has through participation in the Game of Outlaw. Moreover, the Game of Outlaw is reinforced by the strict adherence to it among the young men who constitute it. Speaking of the way he accounts for his life, James described the flexibility he feels around certain constituencies at the Training School compared to the rigidity he feels among his friends: "I feel like I can adapt more with the people trying to help me more than the people that ain't tryin' to help me. 'Cause if I tell my friends, like, the things I'm sayin' now, they'll probably laugh at me. But that's why, like, I don't have a lot of [positive friends]."

The Game of Outlaw seems to present a fairly rigid set of rules and understandings, and young people's deviation from these rules and understandings can easily threaten their status in the game.

CHAPTER TWO

Investment and Pure Critique

Joshua was part of the first group of writers I ever taught at the Training School, and another friend of Anthony's and Jacob's. A Latino from a small working-class neighborhood of Providence, Joshua cut an intimidating figure. He was barely younger than I was, about a hundred pounds heavier, and his long, disheveled curls and five-o'clock shadow made him look even more menacing. Joshua was also seething at the state that had locked him up on drug charges. In our premier issue of *Hidden TREWTH*, he wrote our cover story on the state's Department of Children, Youth and Families (DCYF)—the department that also administers the Training School:

> In critical slang it is known as the Department that Controls Your Families. Reasons vary....DCYF take children away from their families when there is a conflict within the family that may make that family live dysfunctionally. Of course there really aren't any set rules or limits that states what makes a dysfunctional family. Supposedly if your

family aren't happy and...getting along like "Full House" episodes then there is a problem....A child is neglected, call DCYF. A child getting spanked, has marks and bruises, call DCYF....Sounds real good. Why is it thought of negatively?...Maybe DCYF sticks their nose in families who don't need the assistance of the state. Maybe when children and youths enter the system they leave more corrupt than they ever were.

—Joshua, *Hidden TREWTH*, no. 1 (May 2001)

Joshua was also the first young man with whom I connected postrelease. I found him at his mother's house in a neighborhood of Providence. On the day we spent time together, he cooked me a roasted chicken lunch and we played basketball for several hours with his brother at the local park, joking and horsing around. Afterward, with Joshua in the driver's seat, we whipped around the neighborhood to pick up another one of his friends. By the time we got back to his mom's place, a police car was behind us with its sirens on. The four of us got out of the car, as the police proceeded to ask the other three—all people of color—for identification. When I, a white man about the same age as the others, asked if the police wanted to see my identification as well, the police asked, "Were you in that car too?" Several months later, I would find out that Joshua had been rearrested for attempted murder. The rumor was that the victim had been the same brother we had played basketball with that day.

For those most invested in the Game of Outlaw, participation seems to make possible a particular kind of insight into the social world from which the game represents a partial rebellion, an insight that I call a *pure critique*. This perspective on the social world contains a sophisticated understanding of the Game of Outlaw and its relationship to broader society, yet it is an understanding unaffiliated with any kind of change in behavior. This pure critique, then, serves to reproduce young men's marginalization. Joshua's insight into the Department of Children, Youth and Families sits uncomfortably alongside the violence he perpetrated against his own family.

Given the Game of Outlaw's relationship to changes in familial and economic structures observed in the last chapter, it is perhaps unsurprising that many young men's descriptions of their entry into crime relate this entry to the twin pillars of family and economy. The differences in the ways that young men speak of their entries into the Game of Outlaw, however, reveal quite different degrees of espoused investment in it. By investment, I mean both the degree of choice young men feel about participation and the extent to which young men's identities are wrapped up in the game. I do not suggest that those with "low investment" are any less likely to return to criminal involvement than those "highly invested." But *perceived* investment seems quite closely related to different degrees of insight into the social world. Paradoxically, those most invested in the Game of Outlaw—those who perceive very little choice about participation and who identify highly with the game—seem most likely to articulate a pure critique.

LOW INVESTMENT: THE GAME AS DRIFT

Many young men suggested that they had become involved in crime almost by accident. Some understood their initial involvement in crime as a reaction to parents who could not provide them with the support that they needed. For these young people, the Game of Outlaw moved into a vacuum left by the family. Devin, a white young man, connected his involvement in crime to the lack of a father figure: "Since my father wasn't there, my mother bounced. Then I had to be my own father, you know what I'm saying? And in order for me to be my own father... you need like a father figure. You need like the other figure that you look up to growing up. And when you get to that level of being a man, then it's all you. I don't know...the streets was kind of like that father figure. It gave me tools, but I taught myself."

For Devin, the "street" became the father he never had. Other young men connected the absence of family to their initial involvement in crime as well. Robert, an African American, recounted, "My mom had a boyfriend for a long time, and she broke up with him around that same time...I started acting up more too. I think that led towards more of it, cause we used to do more stuff together. After that I'd just be by myself so I started hanging out with my friends more and getting into trouble." It was only after he stopped spending time with his mother and mother's boyfriend that Robert began getting into trouble. This trouble, he remembered, began with a single peer and a lack of interesting alternatives: "My first time I was young, I was chillin' with my boys, and then we met up with some other kid, it seemed like interesting stuff to do, and before I didn't really do anything bad, till I met up with this kid."

After explaining how growing up in a "dysfunctional home made me dysfunctional," Dan, a white young man, went on to describe how he began getting involved in crime "just tryin' to find some love." For Dan, the lack of support from family led to self-described feelings of loss, which he felt compelled to fill with a peer group that led him into trouble: "I didn't have no love in my life, I didn't have my mom or my dad, so I didn't have no one to show me love, so I just grew up not really caring and hatin' a lot of stuff. So as time went on I started chillin' with people I thought that loved me, or showed me love, which I thought was love, but all it was getting me in trouble, and fed up in negative stuff. So I started drinkin' with them and chillin' with them and smoking, among other things we used to do."

For James, instability in his household also led to spending more time with friends, which, in his mind, led naturally to engaging in criminal behavior: "My mom and dad broke up when I was younger, and then my dad was gone for about five years, and then he came back into my life when I was about thirteen or fourteen, but by then I was already hangin' on the streets and most, that's mostly where I grew up. I was at my house from time to time, but most of the time I spent on the streets. So when you're on the streets so much with negative people you start engaging in negative behaviors." In these cases, an absence of family was filled by involvement in crime.

In the stories of another group of young men, participation in crime was a force that overpowered the advice and support offered by family. In these stories, the guilt and personal responsibility felt by residents in relation to their own involvement in crime was most tangible. Malcolm recounted: "I'd say the biggest reason for me coming to the Training School is probably not listenin' to my parents. Their warnings and their stop signs, you know, letting me know the way I was headin'. I've done a lot of things in my life that weren't right, but I think the biggest thing that wasn't right was not following directions from my parents."

Malcolm expressed his gratitude to his parents for warning him against making the decisions he had made nonetheless. Perhaps the memory of his parents' warnings is related to why he himself was so committed to warning others not to make the same decisions, mentioning in our interview the seriousness with which he often discusses his crime with younger friends and family. Malcolm, with the help of his mother, had also been writing a book that he hoped would help other young men stay out of trouble. On the other hand, at a different point in our interview Malcolm referred to feeling a lack of support from his family, then immediately took responsibility for this feeling: "I felt sometimes that I was lonely, I felt like I just, my family wasn't there for me when they actually were, but I wasn't allowing them to be there for me." While he suggested that he has received support from his family, he also acknowledged that he looked for meaning and approval elsewhere. Malcolm explicitly discussed his desire to have his peers look favorably on him:

> I don't know, maybe I felt, some of the things I felt I had to do to impress people, to impress my friends. Sometimes I felt if I didn't do certain things my friends would think different of me. If I necessarily didn't fit in with the crowd then I wouldn't be wanted. So I thought that if I did some of these things that maybe made me look more of a man, or make me be a better friend, or make me look cool because I did these things, instead of thinking about myself and my family I was tryin' to think about impressin' friends and makin' more friends.

Another resident, Frank, engaged similar themes, describing the support of his family and his own irrational response to this support: "Like basically it was just my family, my mother and father, tried to explain to me about the right ways and what I needed to do to keep my life on the right path, and just, friends that I hung out with were saying something different and it was just, you know, you get with your peers and it's like, when you're with people your age you're more apt to listen to them, you know what I mean?...You think older people are old."

Both Frank and Malcolm described their own culpability and responsibility for getting involved in crime, giving in to peer pressure after not heeding their parents' advice. Frank, explaining why he did not listen to the good advice of his parents, suggested that "when you're growing up you want to be the one that's in charge" and said that "nobody could tell [him] nothing." This was the story of an autonomous individual who failed to take responsibility for his actions. Explaining how he hoped to change, Frank continued: "Like there was other stories I used to tell....Blamin' everybody, like I didn't do nothing, it was this person and that person, but then you get older and you realize. You make mistakes. Like I made mistakes, and you just gotta take responsibility for the mistakes that you make."

What is the attraction of the Game of Outlaw for these young men? They tended to describe only the excitement of crime or the bad influence of peers. Robert recounted how he was "chillin' with [his] boys" without causing trouble until they met up with another boy who had "interesting stuff to do." Robert remembered the rush of breaking into a salon with his boys, getting caught, and running to his house and hiding in the closet. Asked why he started hanging out with the boy who got him involved in crime, Robert responded: "Something to do. I was bored. Something to keep me entertained." At another point in the interview, Robert described how his involvement in crime emerged out of laziness, that he has been "laid back and unmotivated," content that "whatever happens happens." Blaine similarly described how he went along with his peers in his initial involvement with crime: "I was with my boys, they saw some guy they didn't like, or whatever, so they figure, 'Hey let's just jump him, take his money and everything.'" Frank described how, in the face of his parents' advice, he was going to do what he wanted to do. And that just led to hanging out and getting into trouble. One of the things he thought caused all the difficulty to come was, "like when you get with a certain group you try to prove yourself, like try to prove to somebody that you're somebody that you're actually not, and that causes a lot of problems too."

One resident connected his involvement with crime to the new social networks he made while attending a new high school in Providence:

Interviewer: How did you start getting into trouble?
Resident: Um, like it all started when I went to Central for like the first year, and like I started hanging around with different people, different crowds, I started meeting all kinds of people, I started getting into gangs and stuff. People like Spanish, Asians, Blacks, you know, all types of people. They were saying, like, you know like, this is the way it should be. I had different friends, but I didn't get along with all of them as much as I did with them.

James described a process through which he got involved in crime despite having had multiple employment opportunities. After a few months spent in the Rhode Island Training School and then being released, James remembered how he "was doing pretty good," that he "had a job and everything." But this situation collapsed as James "started sellin' marijuana, which led me back here last year." Released again, this time from a private treatment program, James found a "good job" in which he felt treated well by the owner. Yet he soon lost this job as well: "I got out last October I had a job, I got a car for my birthday, everything was going good. But after a while, I got, I was working two full-time jobs, I just got sick of it, and I quit the jobs. And I didn't have any money, so I started hanging around with the negative people again, which led me back here by sellin' drugs."

James's criminal activity seemed at least loosely related to the low wages he was paid at these jobs, or to his desire to make more money than he was able, evidenced by his marijuana dealing and, later, by his working two full-time jobs that he ultimately got "sick of." But crime was a substitute for work, in his mind, not an adaptation to an inability to find work. Asked to explain his criminal involvement more generally, he explained, "I was hanging around with gang members and doing activities that wasn't positive to the community but in my eyes it was fun and we enjoyed doing them. I don't know, just to get the adrenaline rush." The excitement of crime—and the meaning he derived from his participation in it—seemed at least as important as the material resources this activity brought him.

The young men who assert individual agency and responsibility for delinquent pasts, then, have to reconcile this agency with the recognition of having been influenced substantially by their peers. Frank's account illustrated this tension clearly:

> I knew everything, nobody could tell me nothing, and so I think that's one of the, that's the main reason what led me here was that, because of the fact that I thought I knew

everything so nobody could tell me nothing, so I was going to do what I wanted how I wanted to do it. And that just led to hanging out and getting in trouble, and another thing I think that caused all this to come on was like, when you get with a certain group you try to prove yourself, like try to prove somebody that you're somebody that you're actually not, and that causes a lot of problems too, and I think, like, growin' up.

In one breath, Frank described how no one could influence him at all. In the next breath, he described how his criminal involvement was closely related to trying to impress his peers.

While this understanding of involvement in crime does show insight into the influence of social networks, and the importance of communities in which to constitute meaning, it does little to elucidate why the resources at stake in the Game of Outlaw are what they are. What makes breaking into a salon and getting chased by the police exciting, instead of participation in a sports league or the pursuit of good grades in high school? What makes illegality more appealing than activities within the boundaries of the law? Absent in these accounts is criticism of any structure broader than the family or peer group, or any examination of the conditions of possibility for the Game of Outlaw itself.

Almost all of these young men portrayed the Game of Outlaw negatively. While they varied in the degree to which they blamed themselves or their families, most of these young men spoke as if they were unattached to their involvement in crime, having "seen the light" either of their own bad decisions or the negative influence that their family situations had on them. In their conversations with me, they expressed hopes that they would be able to extract themselves from the Game of Outlaw upon release.

CONDITIONAL INVESTMENT: THE GAME
AS ECONOMIC CHOICE

Other young men discussed their criminal involvement almost entirely as it related to the material resources for which they strove. Drug dealing may be illegal, but it is a way to secure participation in consumer culture. In this narrative, participation in crime makes economic sense, and almost nothing else about the attraction of the Game of Outlaw is explicitly acknowledged.

The most common narrative explaining criminality among this group is one in which a young man does not want to have to ask his mother for the money necessary to buy what he wants. Luis explained within the first five minutes of our interview why he sold drugs: "I don't like my mom spending money on me, so I like to just make money on my own." By understanding his drug dealing in this way, he made this behavior consistent with his love and respect for his mother—values that seem central to his conception of self. Yet it became clear over the course of the interview that Luis's mother did not consider his drug dealing an act of consideration and that Luis realized this the first time he was sent to juvenile prison: "When I put her through all this, she was crying and all that, so I thought I was doing her a favor by her not spending money on me, but when I got locked up I found out that I wasn't doin' her a favor. 'Cause she, she tells me...'Cause I never even told her, like, I wouldn't even ask for other clothes, 'cause I don't like her spending money. And she was like, 'Even if I don't have it, all you got to do is ask me and I'll find it.' But I can't do that. I love her, and I don't know. I can't put her through that."

Despite his mother's pleading for him to stay out of trouble, however, and his own sensitivity to this pleading, Luis ultimately reiterated his interpretation of his own involvement in drug dealing as a way not to "put his mother through" the hardship of earning the money Luis could earn through his criminal activity.

Rudolfo's understanding of his initial criminal involvement was similarly contradictory with regard to his family. Like Luis, Rudolfo described his involvement as the result of not wanting to put pressure on his mother for money he knew she did not have: "I just got to the age when I was seventeen I started seeing things I wanted, you know what I'm sayin', things I didn't want to bother my mom for, I wanted things on my own, drugs was the thing, that's where money was at so I decided to deal some drugs, know what I'm sayin', made some money here and there."

Rudolfo repeated this sentiment later in the interview, asserting that there were "things he wanted" that he "didn't want to ask his mom for, that she couldn't give [him]." Like Luis, then, Rudolfo attributed his early involvement in crime to a version of consideration for his mother. Yet when I asked Rudolfo about early turning points in his life, Rudolfo responded, "As I grew I started noticing, like, I disrespected my mom, you know what I'm sayin', I just started to do whatever I want. Like the older I got, the more power I felt, like I had to just like do whatever I want. Like I really didn't care, you know what I'm sayin', like, I'm older I can do whatever I want, like disrespect my mom, you know what I'm sayin', that was it." Rudolfo simultaneously seemed to recognize his criminal involvement as emerging out of respect and disrespect for his mother. Embedded in these accounts was the desire to be autonomous young men, who did not need the financial or emotional support of their mothers.[1]

In these accounts, young men minimized the peer group as a source of meaning, while they emphasized the economic benefits of crime. Illegal activity is the only activity that will secure the resources necessary for the physical appearance and material possessions these young men value. About legal work, Rudolfo observed: "Plus some of these jobs they wouldn't hire me too, it's kind of a hassle getting a job, being seventeen, certain places I wouldn't work at, but, just drove me to selling drugs basically, know what I'm sayin', wanted things, getting them, quick money, especially, that's the main thing right there. Having that quick money."

While Rudolfo asserted that there were certain places he "wouldn't work at," it seemed clear that he did try unsuccessfully at one point to secure legal employment. He first blamed a lack of good job options for "driving him" to sell drugs, only then turning to his desire for "having that quick money." Rudolfo suggested that he could have found employment but that this work was below him. In this way he seemed to preserve a degree of free will in his decision to deal drugs. As in James's account, however, it seems likely that this "decision" to deal drugs was at least partially inspired by his relative exclusion from the job market.

Luis spoke about young men's employment decisions more generally in relationship to how he believed Training School staff members wanted young men to behave upon release: "There's very few that will go out there and go straight to jobs, especially after they sold drugs, 'cause going back to making fourteen hundred a week to, to five hundred a week is crazy to think about."

What seemed especially striking about Luis's statement was the assumption that young men could find legal jobs that paid five hundred dollars per week (twelve dollars and fifty cents per hour, given a forty-hour week) if they tried. Like Rudolfo, Luis presented young men's criminality as a choice made consciously between illegal and lucrative work, on the one hand, and legal and less lucrative (but still fairly well-compensated) work on the other hand. In this sense, both seemed to downplay the reality that jobs are *not* easily available for all young men in Providence, that the choice to participate in the illegal economy is in some ways driven by the realities of economic exclusion.

Both Rudolfo and Luis presented their involvement in illegal behavior as the result of a choice *not* to engage in the undignified or less lucrative work available to them. In this sense, they showed a degree of insight into an economic structure that presented them with limited and undignified opportunities to make money legally. Furthermore, their perception of their involvement in crime as a decision to "opt out" of the legal economy might be interpreted as a form of resistance to an economic system that humiliates and degrades the lower class. Yet we might also see this "decision" as an adaptation to an economic system that excludes poor young men even more completely than the young men themselves acknowledged. Young men's decision to opt out clearly does not squeeze the labor supply for Providence's service industry. This decision not to participate in an economy that does not offer room for participation may lead to a psychological reconciliation but certainly does not lead to lasting economic power for young men. Indeed, young men's exit from the legal economy precludes any sort of strategic exercise of voice within this economy and entraps young men in a cycle of crime and incarceration.

Those young men who attributed their involvement in crime to material acquisition alone seemed invested in their own identity as criminals and in their own choices to undertake criminal activity willingly. At one point in my interview with Luis, he rejected the suggestion that "deep down" he might not be a drug dealer by asserting his integrity, a value he attributed to the good parenting of his mother. He saw the suggestion that he was not "really" a drug dealer (a standard liberal line suggesting the possibility of the offender's reform) as an attack on both his own capacity to be true to himself and, by association, on the way he was brought up:

> Like some people say you should try to be you. Like they tell me, "Try to be you. You're not a drug dealer." But I think that I am a drug dealer, this is what I am, I'm not tryin' to be like nobody else. 'Cause my mom taught me, she raised me better than that. She raised me the good way, it was just my mom, six other brothers. And she raised me the right way. I was getting punished, always had a curfew. But it was me who wanted to go out there and sell drugs, no one was holding me back. It wasn't that I wanted to be like somebody, I just wanted my own things. Instead of, like, her spending money on me. I didn't like that.

Two things are worth mentioning here. The first is that it seemed important for Luis to assert his own capacity to choose the life he leads. The second is that his assertion of his capacity to choose his life was connected with the assertion that he was raised the "right way." Again, this interpretation of his upbringing let Luis see his criminal behavior as consistent with the respect he has for his mother. Since he was raised the "right way," he knew he did not have to pretend to be someone he was not, and so his choice to be involved in criminal activity was his and his alone.

Despite these assertions of individual responsibility, there are suggestions of social structure in each of these young men's accounts. On the one hand, they seemed to conceive of themselves as autonomous from social structures and capable of responsible and noncriminal "moral" choices. On the other hand, they seemed to sense the impact of social forces at work in their own behavior, without being able fully to account for these forces. Luis discussed his own previous attempts to "turn around":

> But every time I find myself tryin' to do good, I'll give my good thoughts, and I'll think about doing good, but every time I always find myself thinking of doing a little bit to try to get over. Like I'll say I'm gonna work two jobs if I have to, but then I'll...go to college....But then I'll always find myself thinking, "Maybe I could just sell weed and make some extra money, but I won't be in the streets as much." And I feel like that, like I'll think, and every time I want to do good, something bad pops up, and even if it's just a little bit, I know it ain't the right thing to do, but it's just there, like just tempting me.

Luis described a sort of internal struggle where "good thoughts" compete with "bad thoughts" to influence his behavior. The good thoughts encouraged him to work two jobs and go to school. If he only listened to his good thoughts, he would turn his life around. Yet these good thoughts were overshadowed by bad thoughts, which returned him to crime. To the extent that the question of turning his life around was a question of listening to his own good thoughts, the logic to which Luis subscribed was one of moral responsibility—his crime as evidence of his own depravity. On the other hand, the bad thought was not an "evil thought" but a rational analysis, "doing a little bit to try to get over," a recognition that there was more money in selling weed than in working two low-paying jobs.

Similarly, Rudolfo described how what he "wanted" upon release was undermined by "this little thing" he had about selling drugs. "I wanted to straighten out but yet I always had this little thing about selling drugs you know what I'm sayin', and as soon as I went out there I went back to selling drugs. I was just thinking about it...what I was doing before I was locked up. And when I got out, I went back to doing the same thing what got me in here locked up."

Both Luis and Rudolfo seemed to account for their behavior in terms that mask the social forces at work—the lack of jobs available for young people in Providence, the extraeconomic meaning that both seemed to derive from being involved in the drug trade, and the influences of their peers. Yet they both also described tensions between what they consciously wanted as they were released from prison and what they subsequently did. In this way they hinted at the disjuncture between a moral Game of Law to which they could subscribe in juvenile prison and the Game of Outlaw in which they engaged on the outside.

In these young men's accounts, crime "made sense" as the way to make the most money, to gain access to material advantage and social standing. These young men alluded to social structures when they discussed the lack of alternative jobs, but these social structures were hidden underneath a rhetoric of personal choice.

FULL INVESTMENT AND THE PURE CRITIQUE

Those who attributed their participation in crime to boredom, peer pressure, or the lack of a supportive family failed to account for why criminal activity was the solution to their boredom or was the direction in which peers were pressuring them. Those who attributed their participation in crime to the desire for flashy clothes and fancy cars failed to account for why these accoutrements *mattered* for them. The Game of Outlaw at once offers material and motivational rewards to the young men involved, is a way of getting money and a way of making sense of one's life. This was recognized most completely, ironically, by those who saw crime as intimately tied to both family and economy.

For this third group, entry into the Game of Outlaw did not represent a significant turning point at all. It was, instead, part of the way life had always been. For these young people, initial involvement in crime was actually consistent with, or even a part of, family life. The most powerful account in this respect was Terrence's, who described his siblings' attempt to steal food from his elementary school:

> I'm chillin' with my fam', right, my older heads, we up in the crib, ribs is touching, we hungry man, we like "Yo, ain't nothing to do, ain't no food in the house," know what I mean, ma, we don't know where she was right, she was gone and shit, boom, she was probably workin', mom was good for workin', we just never seen her. Alright, broke into school, whatever, then we just started eatin' cause there's food in there, so we're eating out of the teachers room, just chillin'. I guess some people seen us pop up in there or

whatever, so we come out we greeted by the popos, the cops is right there, they posted up.

In Terrence's account, early criminality was connected with family need. The school, conceived by Terrence's siblings as a resource for which it was not intended, served as a powerful symbolic backdrop, an institution that would never be of much educational service to Terrence. Also of significance was the absence of Terrence's mother, who left Terrence and his siblings behind in order to work.

Harmony, the only young woman interviewed, told a relatively similar story about the tight connection between criminal involvement and her family.[2] She remembered first becoming involved with crime after running away from a bad living situation and finding her brother in New York:

> My brother said if I wanted to run away and be away and shit, if I wanted to be away and not go back to my aunt's house, and not be good, then I would have to do the same thing. And I didn't have anything, and I didn't know anything, so....People in my neighborhood were in gangs and shit, you know, other young kids that I knew and shit. So I just kind of went along too because they were helping them out. It wasn't like necessarily selling drugs at first. It was just like bring shit certain places and then get money for it. So it was easy 'cause it wasn't really like out on the corner and selling drugs, like that. It was just like grab stuff and bring it over there, you know what I mean. Things like that 'cause we's little kids and cops's not gonna bother us.

In a third example, the Game of Outlaw existed even more explicitly *within* the family itself. Some degree of physical confrontation between siblings is not unusual in any family, but when this violence reached the point at which a mother felt forced to call the police, it was reconfigured as criminal—and became a point of entry for this young person into the Game of Outlaw:

> 'Cause last time I got in a fight, right? Near my house, my mom called the cops without me knowing, and the cops came and they arrested me. When I'm the one that got attacked. It was me and my brother fightin'.... It was me and my brother fighting in the house.... My mom called the cops without us knowing after we fought 'cause there was a lot of blood and everything. And when the cops came my brother was scared, but I'm the one that got locked up. They said I had a warrant. I don't trust cops. And then when I...that's when I came here overnight one time, and then I left again. They said it was a mistake. I didn't have a warrant. That pissed me off. I don't trust those cops at all. Cops stole money from me and everything.

In all of these accounts, involvement in crime—and an oppositional relationship to the police—was intimately related to participation in family life. It was a part of what life in these young peoples' families *meant*.

In the same way, these young people equated crime with the legal market from which they have been excluded. Crime was seen as just "another hustle," as Terrence explained: "You can be hustling, you can be workin' a nine to five, that's a hustle in itself, I think that's the strongest hustle right there. That's, that's some, that's hard time right there, workin', man, you wakin' up early, you goin' to work, you come back exhausted, and then on top of that every time you look out the window you see somebody, potential money."

Even when discussing his plans to change his relationship to the Game of Outlaw, Terrence compared it to the legal economy and emphasized the injustice in both: "I was a worker out there, in all aspects of the word, you know? If my peoples needed something that was me, I'd do it. That's how it is. But it's like, it's just like the corporate world, though, 'cause the workers are the first ones to get disregarded when it's time for bonuses, man, they start from the top up. And the workers, we at the bottom, we just keeping stability, that's all. So I noticed that, though. But without the workers, there's no stability. I don't think that anybody realizes that yet."

It seemed like some sort of poetic justice that Terrence's first criminal activity on his own (after breaking into school with his siblings, as described above) involved shoplifting jewelry from local stores, in that jewelry was one of Rhode Island's primary industries prior to the 1970s. Had Terrence been alive forty years earlier, he may well have been working in the jewelry industry. In these accounts, the Game of Outlaw and market were synonymous, or at least symmetrical—the Game of Outlaw just one more way to "make it" in an economy in which everyone is out for themselves.

These young people saw their own involvement in crime as connected both to the support offered by the peer group *and* to the material rewards of this activity. Harmony described her first enchantment with gang activity. Traveling to Las Vegas around the age of twelve, she saw the degree to which gangs exerted their influence in the city: "It made me see that they took over a certain part of a community. And that if I was to regain a certain amount of knowledge about it, I could come back and do the same thing, you know what I mean. Or I could do it within myself, you know what I'm saying, and try to be bigger than what I thought I could be, something like that." Harmony saw both the connection between meaning and material rewards in gang activity—the support that she could derive from gang membership, combined with the power that a collective group of young people could exert in a city.

Terrence, similarly, described his previous relationship to his community as one that combined crime with a type of political consciousness:

Terrence: Before I came to the Training School? Before I came the first time I described myself as, I was a hustler, man. That's what I did. I was sneaky, know what I'm sayin'? I got around things. I was always making money, with dreams of helping the hood. But I really couldn't help the hood, I was just a youngin.

Adam: Could you explain "dreams of helping the hood"?
Terrence: Dreams of helping the hood? Man, just little stuff. Little stuff that gives you the feelin' that you did something, like. Boom. When the ice cream man comes to the hood, and everybody in the hood is going to run up to him. Half the kids ain't got no money, but they going to run up to him anyway. Helpin' the hood, like you go there, know what I'm sayin', . . . you got a little bit of money, you start passin' out ice cream to kids. That fills you with something, that makes you be like, "Yeah," helping these little dudes out, or whatever. It's stuff like that, helping the hood out, man, you see like most of the time when cats is out there clackin', you're also talking to your clients, your customers, you're like, "You don't need to be doin' this," whatever, know what I mean. But they still going to do it, so you still goin' to sell it to them. But you're still tryin' to help out. Like the hood, they fallin' apart up there,

man, they fallin' apart. So, and now, when I'm out, I'll stop by little boo or whatever, maybe I'll declare and be like, "Yo, man, get your life together," 'cause I'm tryin' to push a CD, and I want all these cats on it, I'm tryin' to bring my whole hood with me. I'm bringing up Newport as a whole. I'm not just goin' to eat alone. Either we all eat or we all starve, that's how I move.

Interestingly, Terrence presented himself as a kind of counselor to his own customers, encouraging them to get off drugs at the same time he made money off of their addictions. He went on to describe a sort of democratic pedagogy toward which he strove outside the Training School: "That's the best way to help somebody, you bring them with you. Come on, let's get on the bus, here's how it's gonna be. But you don't give them that plan, that structure where there's one person sittin' on top dictatin'. You let everybody sit around the table together and we all put our say in. So it's like, I'm not telling these cats what to do, I'm tryin' to help them get through it."

While Terrence's involvement in peer groups had evidently led to his trouble with the law, by his account it had also led to a sense of solidarity and participatory decision making characteristic of the healthiest of communities and societies. And while Terrence asserted his desire to get out the Game of Outlaw, his investment in it was also quite clear:

> I don't wanna see nobody end up like Terrence, man, I'm sayin', like, I have a lot of pull, leeway wherever I go, but it's not the life, you know. I don't wanna be sittin' in jail sayin, "I got juice." That don't get me nowhere in life, that's not doing nothing but taking years off of me, putting years on my family, takin' years from me, takin' it to the

free world, donatin' it. "Get up out the hood, man." That's
the best advice I can give anybody, but that's my heart at
the same time, the hood, that's where I'm from, but man,
I'm tryin' to get up out of there though, tryin' to hit up
college, though, for real.

Among these young people, for whom the Game of Outlaw was
intimately related both to the peer group and to the market, the
peer group and family were indistinguishable from one another.

Paradoxically, then, those who saw the limits of their own
agency, and who were most invested in the Game of Outlaw,
had the greatest possibility for the "cognitive liberation"
(McAdam 1982) associated with organized political activity.
These young people saw the Game of Outlaw most clearly for
what it was: an adaptation to the unique social and economic
position of young men in the poorest neighborhoods of the
nation. But as I discuss later, these possibilities were actually
enhanced by the Training School.

Yet these young people's sophisticated critiques of the Game
of Outlaw did not preclude their participation in it. The recognition of the game's intimate relationship with family was used to
justify the constitution of a broad "family" that refuses to "snitch"
while it kills one another. But rather than accuse these young
people of manipulating political ideas for the purposes of continued criminal engagement, a more useful way for thinking
about their understandings is as what Paul Willis (1977) calls a
partial penetration, or what I call *pure critique*. For Willis, the
partial penetration is a type of insight into social structure that,
while accurate, tends to reproduce social structure because of its
partial nature. Willis analyzed working-class boys who rebelled
against the middle-class norms of their schools, romanticizing

instead the macho, working-class lives of their fathers in the factories. While this rebellion represented resistance to middle-class normalization on the one hand, it wound up entrapping another generation of young men in factory work.

What is most significant to me about this perspective is that it represents a critique removed from the realm of action. Broad critiques of society that offer no alternatives for action may actually be counterproductive to one's capacity to live within or to change these structures. More generally, this pure critique locates power as above and separate from young people themselves, as something that they can rebel against but cannot change. One of the favorite books of Training School residents who shared this sort of critique was William Cooper's *Behold a Pale Horse*, a book explaining everything from the cold war to the assassination of Kennedy and the Apollo moon landing as a series of conspiracies undertaken by a shadowy group called the Illuminati. These sorts of conspiracy theories are consistent with a political perspective that is removed from a belief in the capacity of one's own practice to affect the world.

In the next chapter, I will explore how young men's different positions in relationship to the Game of Outlaw were affected by the juvenile prison and the institutional understanding provided by staff there, the Game of Law.

PERSPECTIVE AND POSITION: RACE AND OUTSIDER MASCULINITY

In this chapter I have sought to explore how different levels of espoused investment in outsider masculinity are correlated with different types of insight into the broader social world. I have deliberately refrained from exploring young men's objective positions in the social world. Given the nature of the interviews, it is difficult to explore variation in the relationships between the objective positions young people occupied before entry into the Game of Outlaw and the interpretations they have of these positions.

That being said, those from lower-middle-class families, as opposed to families in deep poverty, seemed more likely to display a low investment in outsider masculinity, while those who entered from deep poverty were more likely to display higher investment. Similarly, white Training School residents seemed less invested than residents of color. This makes some residents much more likely than others to understand their participation in crime as a "role" separate from "who they really are."

The Game of Outlaw takes place in particular neighborhoods, is coded black, and is associated with particular sorts of crime. It seemed easier for white young men living in the suburbs to understand their participation as only a role. Frank, a white young man, had been sent to the Training School six times since 1998 and was initially incarcerated there for sexual assault. How did he find a way of understanding himself *other* than criminal?

> I mean, like, you know, there's people that grew up in the
> environment where it was nothing but selling drugs and
> guns.... But then there's people that see them kind of
> people and like, they think that's the cool way to be, so they
> want to be accepted so they start getting into the sellin'
> drugs and, you know, acting, that gang mentality, just so
> they can fit it. But it's really not, it's kind of destroying

them because it's makin' a character that they're actually not.... Yeah, like basically that's what happened to me. I mean, I've been not really involved in gangs, but I've made attempts to get into gangs and hanging in neighborhoods that, it wouldn't really be hanging in, but.... It's like, I grew up in the country basically. So the city is not something that I would be in.

Frank described how participation in criminal activity represented a break from who he really was:

But the thing with that is sometimes the people that you're likin' aren't really who they are. They're just a character that they're portraying. So you get into it and then you start tryin' to portray yourself as being that kind of person too when you're really not. So basically you lose yourself because you're proving to everybody you're somebody else and you don't really know who you are because you're trying to be this one and then that one and this one, instead of being who you really are.

Frank, like so many in the United States, seemed to see the criminal as the young black man living in the city. Frank could then dismiss his own criminal involvement as "pretending to be someone he was not."

The fact that the initial offense for which Frank was incarcerated was sexual assault may also have contributed to his outsider status vis-à-vis the Game of Outlaw. Among Training School residents, those young people incarcerated for sexual abuse are known as "diddlers" and are chastised. Where sexual conquest was honored, sexual deviance of any sort was looked down upon. As a result, many of these young people tried to downplay the crimes for which they had been incarcerated or to win status among other young people by playing the Game of Outlaw well while incarcerated. Over the course of several months I watched as one young white man in our workshops, incarcerated for sexual abuse, "pledged" with a gang on the inside. Gradually he went from writing poetry about the emotional difficulties of his time in prison to writing poetry about the violence he would inflict on his newfound enemies.

Several of the other white men I interviewed also emphasized the distinction between who they were in the world and who they were when they were playing the Game of Outlaw. Devin remembered:

> Aight, well, I was born Devin Morris, you know what I'm saying. But now it's like, I live by...I don't think it's split personality, but I think people develop a character as they grow up. You know what I'm sayin', they develop a different persona that, which Devin Morris...was just somebody who was doing aight in school and everything like that. Detail's the one that ran the street hustling, making money, you know what I'm sayin', doing whatever and it was like, "I love the streets." I don't know how to explain that neither, but I definitely loved the streets.

Devin was very much aware of the two characters he had played in his life, one that participated in school and the other that took part in the Game of Outlaw. This split persona only seemed attainable among those young men not immediately associated by others with the Game of Outlaw, given their positions as white men.

Martin unconsciously betrayed the racialized nature of the Game of Outlaw as he explained his transition out of it:

Look at all them things I went through, look who I was.
How I used to dress, and how I used to think of myself, and
how I used to talk. Talkin', man, like when I used to talk,
man, the only word you used to catch me sayin' was,
"Nigga." I be like, "Yo, whatup nigga?" I say that right
now, seems like I'm racist, 'cause I haven't said it in so long.
But before, I was just sayin', "What up dog?" I used to say
that so much, I used to be used to it, you know what I'm
sayin'? So nobody who I used to say it to, nobody used to
get offended cause they knew who I was and that's just how
I talk. But I thought I was so, like, thugged out, and that
was just how I talked. I thought I was so real, too, man, but
I was so fake. And I say that now, man, and I'm like, "I feel
offended myself."

Martin described how he used the word *nigga* as a term of
endearment, like so many other young black men, while he
was involved in crime.[3] While he was involved in crime, no
one thought he was being racist since they knew that was
"just how [he] talk[ed]." No longer involved in the Game of
Outlaw, however, Martin was aware that using the word *nigga*
"seem[ed]...racist." Participating in crime seems, in some
way, to have made Martin black. Yet as a white man, he could
choose no longer to be seen as black, could remember his time
as a criminal as "so fake," and could carve out a new identity
that would be more easily acceptable to others because of his
skin color.

Paradoxically, then, it seems to be for those *most* disadvantaged—those born into and enmeshed in the neighborhoods in
which the Game of Outlaw is played; those whose race makes it
difficult to understand themselves as "someone else" when

involved in crime—that there exists the greatest possibility of political consciousness. This consciousness, however, when in the form of a pure critique, merely deepens young men's commitment to a lifestyle that shortens their lives and precludes the possibilities it contains.

PART II

Insider Masculinity

Anthony was hedging his bets when Laura and I began *Hidden TREWTH* workshops at the Training School. Brown University students had come and gone from the facility before, and most residents had learned how to sniff out inauthenticity from a mile away. I felt some pride that, by the publication of our first issue, I had become known as James and the Giant Peach—an effeminate white boy who reminded them of Roald Dahl's zany children's stories. I didn't exactly command their respect, but at least I wasn't pretending to be someone I wasn't.

When we began workshops in the spring of 2001, we imagined creating a space free of the regulations placed on young people within the Training School, as if this absence of regulations itself would lead to freedom. Our first few workshops were co-ed, a rare opportunity for the boys and girls at the facility to interact. This had been part of our attractiveness to administrators, who had come under some pressure from the state for more co-ed programming. The idea, according to one administrator, was to help young men and women begin to have "respectful" relationships with one another.

The workshops were chaotic. One afternoon, when Laura wasn't able to make it, I remember losing control entirely, and I wound up sitting in a corner of the classroom while residents played soccer with a trash can. More often, we'd have moments of creative synthesis that would deteriorate into madness. Our lesson plans were often either wildly overambitious and abstract or nonexistent. Still, in those first months, residents kept coming back, week after week.

Months later, Anthony told me one reason why. Some young men had apparently convinced or coerced a few young women into performing sexual acts on them. Unbeknownst to us, the young men (who made up a majority of the class) had constructed a system in which a couple of them would block our view of the goings on behind them. Our early attempts at establishing a different sort of space at the Training School, then, were likely making possible the worst sort of sexual exploitation. We quickly learned that the absence of all regulations, on which we had initially prided ourselves, had created a kind of vacuum that the Game of Outlaw was able to occupy.[1]

The Rhode Island Training School, the state's only juvenile correctional institution, presents a new environment for young men involved in the Game of Outlaw, a new arena in which they must work to make sense of and gain power over their lives. A point system, based on residents' compliance with institutional rules, regulates the distribution of privileges. Informal alliances with staff also determine a resident's quality of life. Many of the resources over which young people compete (money, turf, standing with women) are simply not relevant in this juvenile prison, while other resources (small class sizes, diverse social networks, "behavioral points" that regulate privileges) affect young people's behavior and understandings in new ways.

The Training School puts forward a new game, a new system of rules and rewards, that young men must negotiate. I call this game the *Game of Law*. This game conflates the goals of rehabilitation and the management of order, encouraging residents to be responsible young men through obedience to often arbitrary organizational mandates. Masculinity is still very much at stake in the Game of Law, but it is a conception of masculinity derived from those men with institutional power. Staff members consciously and unconsciously try to teach residents to accept their subordination in the broader social world—rewarding them for learning to be disciplined and obedient subjects, for enacting what I call *insider masculinity*.

Young men respond to the Game of Law in different ways. Some young men simply bring outsider masculinity to juvenile prison, using prison time to reinforce their status in the Game of Outlaw and to reinforce their commitment to it. As one author wrote:

> Yah face stay the same
> Only the places change
> We locked up so now there's different rules to the game.
> —Shy Boy, *Hidden TREWTH*, no. 15
> (September 2004–January 2005)

Other young men accept the Game of Law and try to become men on the terms of the Training School. In the intersection between the Game of Outlaw and the Game of Law, however, new possibilities exist for political understandings and political organizing.

CHAPTER THREE

Insider Masculinity and the Game of Law

The Training School looks and feels like a mix between a high school and a prison. The school building and campus look like any number of Providence high schools, aside from the tall arched fence preventing escape. This appearance, however, belies a more fundamental confusion about the purposes of the facility—a confusion experienced by teachers, staff, and administrators alike. While rhetorically committed to the idea of "rehabilitation," most adults working at the facility seem hard-pressed to articulate what this means in the lives of young people, whether in their time at the facility or their time postrelease. This confusion is not, by any means, unique to the Training School. Since 1950, there has been collective disillusionment in the capacity of asylums, or "total institutions," to treat those in their care. In the face of this disenchantment, however, the Training School attempts to enact an insider masculinity of work and family life different from the outsider masculinity of the Game of Outlaw.

SITUATING THE GAME OF LAW

An 1895 report on the Training School's predecessor, the Sockanosset School for Boys, reveals the variety of vocational training
in which young men were engaged:

Carpenters' shop	8
Blacksmiths' shop	16
Masons' shop	12
Machine shop	8
Engineers' department	5
Printing office	14
Shoe shop	9
Tailors' shop	12

Regardless of the success with which young people were rein-
tegrated in reality, this focus on vocational training made sense
at a time when industrial labor was needed and jobs were waiting
for young men upon release. Even several decades later, the
superintendent of the school would assert in the *Providence
Journal*, "Wayward boys are a social and not a criminal
problem." He continued, "Eighty per cent of the boys at
Sockanosset...are either foreign born or born of foreign
parents" ("Sockanosset Head Defends 'My Boys,'" *Providence
Journal*, March 16, 1926, 19). Getting to the root cause of delinquency was as simple as slowing the flow of immigrants. The
Immigration Act of 1924, which put caps on immigration, the
superintendent viewed as "the biggest thing we could have done
to reduce juvenile delinquency....We need not care how many
[immigrants] come if they only come slowly enough to give us
time to assimilate them. The nation got indigestion." Sockanosset, and later the Training School, would help assimilate new

immigrant men, help them learn to be workers in an economy that needed them.

The Training School is one manifestation of an organizational form that has existed in the United States since the late eighteenth century. Erving Goffman (1961: xiii) defined this organizational type as an "asylum," as "a place of residence and work where a large number of like-situated individuals, cut off from the wider society for an appreciable period of time, together lead an enclosed, formally administered round of life." The technologies used by asylums are ambiguous and their results are difficult to measure, meaning that their survival depends almost entirely on how they are perceived as complying with unstated norms or rules (Meyer and Rowan 1977).

Regardless of the social purposes these organizations actually serve, then, examining how these types of organizations are legitimated is a window into the norms and values of the era within which they exist. In the early twentieth century, the juvenile prison embodied the norms of Progressive Era elites: their attribution of delinquency to cultural difference and "indigestion"; their optimism about the effectiveness of rational bureaucracy and the ability of the state to mold or "cure" individuals; their faith in industry as salutary.

Of course, these organizations served other important if less overtly recognized purposes. Their prevalence in early twentieth-century America has been explained as an elite response to fears of urban disorder (Rothman 1971), as a form of social control meant to assimilate new immigrants and to train a labor force for the emerging industrial economy (Scull 1977), and as the result of the organizing efforts of new professions such as psychiatry and social work (Platt 1969). More broadly, the "rehabilitative consensus" (Garland 2001) was likely sustained by a manufacturing economy that tightened labor supply and made criminal populations potentially valuable as workers, and by a rigid social structure that produced compliance (Rusche and Kirscheimer 1939; Young 1999).

The Sockanosset School for Boys, then, did seem to foster a particular conception of masculinity for the boys that it housed, but this conception was intimately tied to the trades into which it intended to integrate its young men. A very different proposition awaits the young men who occupy the Training School today. For one, the school has no illusions about training its residents for useful trades. Indeed, the focus of the Training School has shifted from teaching industrial practices to inculcating proper attitudes. This makes the study of masculinity in juvenile prison all the more interesting. Where at one point prison masculinities were embedded in work practices, proper male attitudes are now taught directly, abstracted from the jobs or job skills to which these attitudes might be applied in practice.

What is responsible for this shift in emphasis? Between 1950 and 1980, as many scholars have observed, social and economic transformations rendered the criminal economically insignificant, while making the middle class more insecure and thus susceptible to a politics of fear (Garland 2001; Young 1999). Moreover, the social-welfare state embodied by the "rehabilitative consensus" was inconsistent with an economy now dependent on an insecure (and thereby "flexible") labor force. The political upheaval of the 1960s and substantive gains made by African Americans during the civil rights movement also played a role in this transformation, setting the stage for a "rights-based" understanding of the role of government, and, in reaction

against the victories of the civil rights movement, a white refor-
mulation of new strategies for racial domination.

The end of the rehabilitative consensus had an internal logic
as well, as specific critiques were leveled in both intellectual and
political fields at the failures of the asylum to fulfill its stated
purposes. Those on the left came to see the asylum as little more
than a way for an oppressive state to discipline those elements
of the population most threatening to it (Goffman 1961; Becker
1963). In its 1971 report, *Struggle for Justice*, the American
Friends Service Committee attacked the longstanding progressive consensus, asserting, "Most if not all of the assumptions that
underpin the treatment model are unsubstantiated or in conflict
with basic humanitarian values" (AFSC 1971). For those on the
right, the public asylum's rehabilitative aims came to be seen
as naive and ineffective attempts to shape deeply ingrained
individual pathologies, a view that found support in Robert
Martinson's oft-cited article in *The Public Interest*, "What works?—
Questions and Answers about Prison Reform" (Martinson 1974).
While the left and right could agree on the failure of the asylum,
the way they interpreted this failure was quite different.

What has replaced an earlier focus on vocational training is
a derivation of the more managerial orientation of adult corrections (Feeley and Simon 1992), through which a facility's success
is judged on increasingly self-referential indicators. Inside a
facility, this means that the maintenance of order and reduction
of resident incidents takes high priority. Outside, this means that
"success" is judged by former residents' compliance with the
tracking practices of the state—clean drug tests, attendance at
drug-treatment or drug-testing centers, and so on. This focus
on discipline for its own sake, however, is understood through

the lens of treatment. Administrators and staff believe that they are inculcating young men with the values they need to be "good men," and at the same time these values help with the daily management of the facility.

The explicit teaching of a male disposition was most apparent to me during a short-lived experiment at the Training School, when the director of the Department of Children, Youth and Families tried to implement a comprehensive "resocialization" program modeled on a similar effort in Texas. The program articulated explicitly what kind of man the facility was hoping to produce. Implemented in full, the plan would have regulated young men's behavior and monitored their cognitive processes much more thoroughly than anything in Training School history. Staff at the facility would have been given discretion over when residents were ready for release, a proposition that was not popular with the juvenile court. As a part of this initiative, for a period of about two years, a series of "thinking errors" were posted on walls around the facility. Among these errors were the following:

> Acting Helpless: Feeling sorry for yourself; saying, "I can't"; asking for unnecessary help; acting like you're the victim and/or wanting people to feel sorry for you.
>
> Overreacting: Having a strong emotional reaction, especially anger, when criticized or confronted; using anger to control others; and/or using emotion to take the focus off the real issue. (Texas Youth Commission: 4.40–4.42)

Through these "thinking errors," young men were instructed to be responsible and unemotional, were told not to get people to "feel sorry" for them. Staff were supposed to hold young men accountable to these standards of thought and action, and some juvenile program workers and teachers were beginning to be trained in running "encounter groups" in which groups of residents would discuss their weekly indiscretions.

What seems to have remained consistent throughout the facility's history is a questionable capacity to achieve its stated goals. Even according to the administrators at the Training School, the facility rarely "works," if we understand this to mean that young men stay out after release. But getting a clear picture of basic recidivism rates at the school is no easy task. At the age of eighteen, juveniles become adults and, if incarcerated, are sent to the Adult Correctional Institution. Yet 77 percent of the 262 young people held at the Training School at the beginning of 2008 were between sixteen and twenty, making it likely they would be adults by the time of next arrest.[1] Moreover, at the age of eighteen, juveniles' records are cleared by state law, which makes it nearly impossible to tell whether those incarcerated at the Training School go on to spend time incarcerated in the adult system. This is compounded by the small size of the state of Rhode Island, which means that young people may easily cross state borders, possibly getting involved in other states' juvenile justice systems without reoffending in Rhode Island. Again, the frequency of this interstate offending is unknown, making recidivism even more difficult to ascertain.

That being said, what the Training School does know is that on December 31, 2002, 67 percent of the 326 young people in its care and custody had been admitted to the facility at least twice; 19 percent had been admitted four times.[2] An in-house study (Little and Abbate 1996) conducted by administrators in the facility found that low-risk, first-time offenders incarcerated in the minimum-security building had a recidivism rate of

between 15 and 16 percent within a period that (due to meth-
odological constraints) varied from five and a half months to
thirty months. An additional 19 percent of offenders were
detained one or more times but were not readjudicated or convicted. Among staff at the Training School's regular facility,
however, estimates of recidivism rates are much higher. One
juvenile-program worker reported that between 70 and 75
percent of young people typically return. Another estimated the
recidivism rate at between 80 and 85 percent.

POINTS, LEVELS, AND COMPETITIVE ACQUISITION

The Game of Law, as typically played, focuses much more
extensively on behavior than on dispositions. This game conflates rehabilitative assumptions with managerial prerogatives
and works to foster an insider masculinity of responsibility,
respectability, and obedience. In this game, the rules are conflated with the stakes, as points are rewarded based on compliance. The larger purpose of the Game of Law is rarely discussed.
Scholars have recognized this conflation elsewhere in traditionally treatment-oriented criminal justice programs (Lynch 2000).

Asylums, however, have always had difficulty measuring organizational success and have always tended to conflate internal
order with "rehabilitation." Michel Foucault (1977) recognized
the relationship between systems of control and the ideas or
knowledge enabled by this control. In Foucault's panoptical
prison, the illusion of perpetual surveillance—a "penality that
traverses all points and supervises every instant in the disciplinary institutions [and that] compares, differentiates, hierarchizes,

homogenizes, excludes"—would lead to normalization (1977: 183), simultaneously constructing and controlling the prisoners' "souls."

What distinguishes the Game of Law from the panoptical gaze is the former's focus on *bureaucratic* as opposed to subjective processes. The souls of inmates are not at stake. Inmates are categorized, but on the basis of the extent to which they comply with rules to make management of the facility easy. At the Training School, a level system is used to determine privileges and to maintain behavior and dominates the daily routines of young people.

According to a pamphlet handed out to residents upon their arrival,

As a level TWO, you are entitled to, at least, the following:

- One phone call a week and unlimited calls to your family court lawyer, CANTS [Child Abuse and Neglect Tracking System], or the federal court lawyer
- One visit a week—parent/guardian, grandparents, siblings, and own children
- Lights out at 9:30 P.M.
- One special visit per month to be arranged with unit manager

As a level THREE, you are entitled to, at least, the following:

- Two phone calls per week and unlimited calls to your family court lawyer, CANTS, or the federal court lawyer
- Two visits a week
- Lights out at 10:30 P.M.
- Walkman in room
- Eligible for on-grounds work

As a level FOUR, you are entitled to, at least, the
following:

- Three phone calls per week and unlimited calls to your
  family court lawyer, CANTS, or the federal court lawyer
- Lights out at 10:45 P.M.
- Walkman in room
- Three visits per week—in addition to the above visitors,
  you may also have girlfriend, boyfriend, aunts/uncles,
  pending clearance. Visitors under eighteen must have
  parental permission.
- Personal blanket
- Community passes if approved by Reclassification Board,
  superintendent, and family court judge

If dropped to level ONE, expect the following:

- No posters on walls
- No phone calls, with the exception of calls to your family
  court lawyer, CANTS, or the federal court lawyer
- One visit per week, from parents/guardians only
- Bedtime at 8:00 P.M., lights out at 8:30
- No store orders/must use state hygiene supplies
- No food or soda during visits
- No extra recreation time

Points are won and lost at the behest of teachers and juvenile-
program workers, who give young people up to 100 points per
week. While the point system sounds like a bureaucratic and
impersonal way of regulating behavior, staff and teachers exercise a great deal of discretion in the awarding of points, meaning
that the system is itself embedded in the personal relationships
between staff and residents.

The point system did seem to elicit investment from at least some residents at the facility:

Interviewer: Is the point system good?
Resident: Yeah, it keeps us in check, really. It keeps us honest and you know keeps us...responsible for how we act. I mean, if I keep my levels, after six months, I might be able to get out anyway. That's good. I mean, it'll give me a chance to...to redeem myself. It's something to work for. That's so important to me.

Playing the Game of Law lets young men prove to themselves and to the staff at the Training School their intention to change, to "redeem" themselves.

DISCIPLINARY POWER

Yet by what standards do staff members award points? Again, unlike the panoptical gaze, there is no central node—spatially or metaphorically—from which young men are observed. Points are awarded almost evenly by teachers and juvenile-program workers, during the school day and in the residential buildings respectively. The different demographics, different organizational prerogatives, and different physical locations of these different staff members mean that they emphasize different facets of insider masculinity and grant points based on different criteria.

Staff positions at the Training School are strictly segregated by sex. Of the juvenile-program workers on record in December of 2006, thirty-five were male and only five were female (many of these female juvenile-program workers likely worked in the young women's facility). Of social workers on record, ten were female and only three were male. Of the teachers on record (for which some records were missing), six were female and none were male. The percentage of juvenile-program workers who were people of color was also significantly higher than the percentage of teachers of color.

Before and after business hours, young men are supervised by mostly male juvenile-program workers, or guards, who emphasize strict obedience to behavioral rules. During the day, on the other hand, young men are supervised largely by women—teachers, social workers, and other professionals—who ask them to "show respect" and be in touch with their emotions.

Perhaps because of the primary importance of security within the Training School, juvenile-program workers have a significant degree of organizational power in the facility (Pfeffer 1981). Juvenile-program workers monitor young men after school hours and are summoned into the classroom when there is disruption. They are implicitly left to define a large piece of the treatment program of the Training School, especially in the residential units, which are geographically separate from the school building. The superintendent of the Training School, the highest ranking staff person on site, is directly responsible for the unit managers and juvenile-program workers in charge of the security of the facility. During the time I worked at the Training School, this superintendent spent significantly more time responding to juvenile-program worker issues than issues to do with the teaching or social-work programs. Teachers report to a separate principal, who is below the superintendent, and social workers likewise report to a chief social worker below the superintendent. Juvenile-program workers are also significantly better compensated than either teaching or social-work positions.

Juvenile-program workers tend to measure residents' success in observable terms, like the order with which young people march or the number of disciplinary warnings that must be issued. This sort of incentive system works well to maintain order in the facility. Most staff interviewed for this study, however, believed that this regime conditioned young people to behave upon release. Rehabilitation and discipline were conflated in several interviews. Said one juvenile-program worker,

> Being in this closed environment where you can't leave, you have to reeducate yourself, you know, reform to what we're doing. And a lot of the residents do. And in doing so…you know, it takes a little discipline to do it—self-discipline and discipline on our part for them to do it. But when they do it, they adjust to it a lot better, and they know, you know, that it's better for them to do it. You know what I mean? It'll benefit them in the long run. You know, they can distinguish that really good. So that's why I think that, you know, discipline is an important part out here, 'cause [if] we don't discipline them, we just let them do what they want to do, then it's just like hanging around, you know what I mean? It's just like no rehab.

Another juvenile-program worker described more explicitly the maturation process many young people went through as they acclimated themselves to the disciplinary standards of the Training School:

> So every time they return, you can see the maturity. You know, first they came in, they're level one their whole bid. Their next bid, they're level two. Their next bid, they're

level four, you know. It's weird to see that. But, you know, they get the mainstream of this whole place and they figured out that, "Hey, this is what they're expecting from me, and this is what I'm supposed to be doing to get out. And this time I'm gonna do it. I'm gonna, you know, try to get out early."

Maturity, this staff member suggested, should be defined as the ability and willingness of young people to play by the rules of the facility, rules that require unquestioning compliance. A third staff member explained the importance of behavioral conditioning in more detail:

You have to condition them. In some units here we have conditioned a lot of these kids ... from walking with their hands behind their back, you know what I mean, knowing where they have to line up when they get outside the door. And yeah, some of the behaviors, they're implanted, but it's just the consistency of doing that on a daily basis that's gonna make any of that successful in regards to their behavior.

What lesson is taught by walking with one's hands behind one's back, by raising one's hand to go to the bathroom? For this staff member, the relationship between behavioral conditioning on the inside and success on the outside was clear: "And it's conditioning kids to understand that certain things in life you have to do, you have to ask before you do. And that's what we try to establish here is getting kids doing things the way they're supposed to be done and following rules. And holding them accountable, which on the outside...a lot of people don't hold them accountable."

It was clear from these interviews how central the idea of discipline was to all three juvenile-program workers' conceptions of resident success. For these staff members, the process of "treatment" was exactly the same process that led to easy management of the facility.

The juvenile-program workers interviewed for this study were likely more progressive and more invested in treatment than the typical juvenile-program worker, given their willingness to speak with me and the fact that I had relationships with many of them before the interviews. Yet even these staff did not feel like the contributions they were making to treatment were valued. One staff member, perhaps the most well-liked among residents, spoke about the paternal role he played:

Staff member: They cling onto you like you're their older brother, or they look to you as a father figure. And it's great because we are in a position to change these guys' lives. And we're not too much seen as that here, you know. We got a bad rap. But...

Adam: Can you talk about that a little?
Staff member: You know, just being a regular guard I guess, you know what I mean? Like we have no feelings and just want to pass down discipline and we're not trying to fix behavior. But that's not true. I see a lotta guys here who, I mean, put their whole heart and soul into a kid, and the kid turn around and do 'em bad, and, you know the guy not looking down on the kid like, "Screw you kid. You did me wrong. Blah blah blah blah."

This staff member was aware of his importance to the young men with whom he worked yet also recognized that he was not afforded much respect among other types of staff. Another juvenile-program worker explained in detail how segregated JPWs were from the more rehabilitation-oriented staff, and therefore how they were denied the sort of information about residents to which other staff had access: "And I think that's one of the problems we have dealing with [residents]. Especially in direct-care staff, is that we don't have enough information on their backgrounds that would probably be beneficial to us to help deal with these kids on a daily basis. Being direct-care staff, that we do deal with them day in and day out, more than anybody in this facility, so that would definitely be a help, you know." While juvenile-program workers felt that their disciplinary role was rehabilitative, they also observed that this rehabilitative function went unrecognized and unaided by a majority of staff at the facility.

Those staff positions most directly concerned with education and the provision of social services, on the other hand, were most often occupied by women. Perhaps this explains why Rodney referred to a female resident when he described what he understood rehabilitation to be: "But my definition of rehabilitation is that, like, adults, some of them even our age go in there and tell them, 'Yo, this is out there. This is out there. You could be modeling. Or you're a nice looking girl. You could be doing this instead of prostitute.'"

Teachers, a vast majority of whom are female, had a different emphasis when discussing the standards of behavior by which they rewarded points than their male juvenile-program worker counterparts. Where the juvenile-program workers seemed to view themselves as father figures, teaching obedience with tough love, teachers seemed to see themselves as women for whom the young men must learn to act like gentlemen. Discussing the "training" of the Training School, then, one teacher focused less on obedience and more on "manners," alongside the basic skills that they felt they could impart to their charges: "Maybe if they learn manners, or maybe if they learn that there's other options out there for them, maybe they won't come back. I think that's what a lot of teachers hope for, I really do. I mean if a kid can read and write, then he's gonna go a lot farther than one who couldn't read or write. Now he could fill out an application. Now he can at least get a job where he'll know how to read and not be embarrassed."

In teachers' minds, there *are* jobs for these young people, if they would only learn basic skills and abandon the Game of Outlaw. This same teacher put it this way: "There are jobs in demand such as electricians and these kids, it's the hands on. They could do that, and there are a lot of places that will take them on as apprentices and pay for them to go to school. And those kids sometimes don't realize stuff like that. Or like the same thing with mechanics. And some of them are really good with computers…you know, getting into a program that has computers and working with computers. "

Rather than understanding young men's dispositions as an adaptation to a social world that has provided them with limited options, teachers suggested that young men must "learn respect" and "realize the options" that have been there all along. Another teacher said, "It's an uncomfortable feeling to look in the mirror and say, 'Wow, I really need to work on, you know, being more compassionate to people.' That's a sign of weakness to them.…

And also the whole pecking order in the units, as far as [if] you're in maximum security, you're supposed to act a certain way. And if you're not portraying yourself in this way, then you become the target of, you know, you're the sissy."

This teacher, unlike any of the juvenile-program workers interviewed, seemed to understand the relationship between emotionality and femininity in the Game of Outlaw. "Being compassionate" leads to you being "called a sissy." But the teacher's focus on training individual young people to show compassion flew in the face of her implicit sociological understanding of young men's resistance to doing so.

Interestingly, then, we see different conceptions of insider masculinity emerge out of juvenile-program workers' and teachers' interviews, each correlated with these staff members' daily practices. For juvenile-program workers, obedience *is* rehabilitation. For teachers, respectful classroom participation seems all that young men need in order to succeed.

But when asked for specific examples of "success stories," or accounts of those young men they observed being "rehabilitated," these stories were few and far between for juvenile-program workers and teachers alike. Five of the six staff members interviewed mentioned the same young African American man (three of the six also mentioned one or two other successes). Having been incarcerated at the Training School, this particular former resident was admitted to a cooking program at Johnson and Wales University and ended up enlisting in the military and fighting in Iraq. Pictures of this former resident were once displayed in the main hallway of the school building, the young man proudly standing in uniform, an enormous gun slung across his shoulder. All residents taking classes walk by these pictures every day.

That five of the six staff members interviewed spoke of the same young man suggests the limited number of successes on which staff can draw. But the fact that this young man became a soldier also seems important. The soldier—disciplined, clean-cut, the epitome of violent tendencies focused on legitimate ends—should serve as the role model. This is all the more ironic when so many residents compare to warfare their daily lives on the streets of South Providence. One teacher, speaking of success stories, mentioned the same soldier alongside another young man who had found a different way to channel violence into acceptable form: "They have both been male, that I can talk about that, since I've been here, I think have been probably the most successful. And one of them went into boxing. You know, professional, semi-pro boxing. And he just was on a regimented ...he had a coach and a really disciplined program. And he's doing extremely well, you know, as far as his career."

Success, for these staff members, seemed most often to be represented by young men who channeled violence into socially legitimate arenas. The only released resident I interviewed who was referenced during staff discussions of success stories was Martin, a resident who found religious faith during his time in the Training School and had become a youth minister. One juvenile-program worker described him this way, "We had a resident that got in, you know, found God while he was here, and now he's working hard. He got married. He actually—he was a rapper while he was here—now he's put God into his rap. He's rapping about God and change and peer pressure and a lot of things like that that these guys need to hear from their peers, which is great." Martin seemed to embody an idealized reentry into the fields of work and family, a reentry made possible by faith.

The ideal man channels the Game of Outlaw into disciplined and accepted arenas. He becomes a soldier, a boxer, a minister. He turns his violence into a legal profession or "raps about God." He gets married.

ORGANIZATIONAL CRACKS AND FISSURES

Despite the close supervision of residents, the control wielded by administration and staff at the facility is inevitably only partial. The failure of the resocialization program, alluded to at the beginning of this chapter, illuminates the discord and disorganization among staff over program goals and implementation. In the above section, I explored the slightly different standards of success by which staff at the facility measure residents. This disagreement only exacerbates difficulties involved in implementing a coherent and comprehensive disciplinary regime within an organization like the Training School. Interviewed in December of 2003 about the resocialization program, few staff felt confident they knew the full story about it. One juvenile-program worker said, "I really can't discuss the resocialization program. I know that we try to implement it in what we do out here, but I don't know how well it's working. So I really would rather not discuss it because I don't wanna throw stones or, you know, accept it. And I really don't know the whole piece, 'cause we haven't really been trained for the whole piece."

Another juvenile-program worker responded, "It's a great program, and I know it's worked in Texas. And we're in the first stages of resocialization. So I don't know too much about it cause we're in the process of training, different classes and everything like that, but seems like a good program."

Finally, a third juvenile-program worker responded with more evident frustration:

> We start things around here. We don't follow 'em through, we don't finish....When you bring in this program, they spend a lot of money getting us trained or starting to train us on this program. Is the program a good program? Well, you know, they made the decision to train us so they must've felt pretty good about it....It was in place for a very short, short period of time. It didn't have enough time to really take off and to see any success out of it. It was just money wasted again....They took a program from another state. That doesn't mean it's gonna work here, you know? ...There's not much to say about resocialization anymore because it's not here.

Teachers also seemed confused about the status of the program. One teacher responded that resocialization had been "temporarily put on the back burner because of, I think funding, and because of inability to get case workers and other workers to get relieved to do different trainings and run groups." Another teacher described her frustration with the program, implying that family court judges were the barrier to implementation: "Or seeing programs such as last year, the resocialization, which was supposed to be this wonderful thing that works great in Texas, but okay, you know, Texas is conservative, we're a very liberal state. We don't have the backing of the judges. There was no way that thing was gonna even work. So why did we waste our time?"

An administrator responded to a question about the program by saying sharply, "That doesn't exist." She further explained that the Training School intended to implement the program, but that to do so successfully the facility would have had to focus on the clinical or psychological aspect of it. Since clinical social workers did not have the time or resources to begin practicing resocialization, this administrator acknowledged, "In my mind, it never existed, nor do I see any hope for it ever to exist without a lot more resources here." Another barrier seemed to be the courts. Based on references to family court judges by both the teacher quoted above and a unit manager, it seemed that the courts were reluctant to shift to a sentencing structure in which discretion was given to the Training School regarding release dates. In reference to this sort of sentencing structure, a unit manager explained, "The courts aren't going to agree to that right now because they don't have the faith" that the Training School will use this discretion justly.

The Rhode Island Training School seems to exist in the middle ground between the chaos of more punitive juvenile corrections systems and the rigid disciplinary regime that the resocialization model strives to achieve. In the most chaotic institutions, the Game of Outlaw becomes magnified on the inside—as young people are brought into close contact with one another without the introduction of alternative institutional understandings. This is supported by evidence that gang boundaries solidify in these institutions in the interest of self-protection. Allegations of staff abusing young people are common as well, when guards—faced with this magnified game—become an exaggerated version of the police force.[3] On the other extreme, however, where a "rehabilitative" or "resocialization" model is exercised forcefully, intensive treatment and programming occupy nearly every waking hour. In these facilities, young people have little freedom to interact with one another, and most interactions are closely supervised.[4]

This middle ground of the Rhode Island facility might be attributed to a number of factors. On the one hand, the size of the state's entire juvenile corrections system is fairly small, especially when compared to the size of systems in places like California. The staff and administration in Rhode Island can strive for standard programming and strict disciplinary regimes, even if these aspirations are undermined by their own divisions and their tumultuous relationship with the courts and outside advocacy groups.

Different people in different positions at the facility explained this lack of a coherent program in different ways. A juvenile-program worker suggested that competing constituencies try to play a power game when they should be concerned with the well-being of the young people they serve:

> Some people just want to seem like they're gonna be the person making this decision and there may be a lot of people that don't agree with that decision but they'll make the decision just because those people don't agree, you know? So there's a lot of egos and a lot of mind games played over here. And they're playing in the wrong field. You know what I mean? This ain't the field you want to play that game on. Certainly because we're supposed to be setting an example and setting precedents for how we're gonna do business.

For a head administrator, the problem seemed as much to do with the difficulty of observing employees. From teachers to juvenile-program workers to social workers, none of the employees who work most closely with residents can easily be observed by the administrators responsible for hiring and firing decisions:

> I think that because there's no oversight of a lot of the employees, there isn't a real strong feeling on the part of everyone to sort of police themselves and do what they're supposed to do. And then because there's not a lot of supervisors or leadership, what happens is that people are in there in their own little worlds. And I don't fault them all the time for it, but they begin to take control of their own little world for survival reasons. And they're running it the way they see fit. And so you end up with a lot of individual little pieces and there's not that consistency, there's not that communication.

As opposed to the analysis of the juvenile-program worker, who attributed inconsistencies to high-level administration, this administrator suggested that the incentives created by a lack of supervision of staff and middle managers created the environment of miscommunication that both she and the juvenile-program worker recognized.[5]

The Game of Law does indeed seem compromised by the realities of the staff's daily management of the facility, which depends on informal alliances struck with residents, and implies a certain degree of acceptance of (and even adherence to) the rules of the Game of Outlaw. Staff members form relationships and make compromises with young people as a part of their work and even co-opt some of those pieces of the Game of Outlaw that serve their own interests (Sykes 1958). Rudolfo recounted, "Staff they're cool, as long as you don't do things you know you're not supposed to do, they won't hit you off, know that I'm sayin', basically it's like, in here, they won't hit you off for every single thing, I don't think any of these buildings will hit you off for every single thing, but if you do something that you know you're going to get hit off, then expect the consequences."

At another point in the interview, Rudolfo highlighted the importance staff place on residents "not act[ing] up when there's guests in the building," implying different behavioral standards for young people when staff are not themselves being observed. Rudolfo suggested a level of discretion in staff members' enforcement of the rules that, while not surprising, runs in opposition to the actuarial approach to discipline suggested by the point system. Luis explained the reasons for staff flexibility even more explicitly: "I think, I think the JPWs [juvenile-program workers] respect you more than the teachers 'cause they're [the teachers] not with you twenty-four seven, and the teachers...You try to mess up, and they try to yell at you and, in a way they try to punk you off, cause they know you can't do nothing, and if you do try to do something the JPWs will come runnin' in there. But I think the JPWs give you more respect than the teachers would."

Implicit in his explanation was the fact that juvenile-program workers have to learn to negotiate with residents, given that they are around residents all the time and have no higher authority to appeal to if order is disrupted. Teachers, meanwhile, are not as enmeshed in the daily lives of young people and could "punk you off" because they could fall back on the authority of the juvenile-program worker. There seems to be a degree of reciprocity in the relationship between young men and the staff. Staff members will not enforce every rule strictly, so long as young men agree to maintain a level of order that does not get staff in trouble. Most generally, given staff members' goal of maintaining order at the facility, strict enforcement of the rules must be balanced against their relationships with young men. Informal alliances with residents provide the scaffolding on which enforcement of the rules is possible.

While juvenile-program workers are supposed to be the enforcers of the Game of Law, then, a second boundary sometimes seems to exist between the young men and juvenile-program workers, on one side, and the other staff and administration on the other. Two of the four juvenile-program workers interviewed explicitly referenced their involvement in crime at some point in the past. A third referenced growing up in the neighborhoods in which many of the young people at the Training School lived. One juvenile-program worker went so far as to equate young men's incarceration with the lack of freedom that juvenile-program workers felt on the job: "It's not the best place in the world to be, especially not in the summer or in the winter for that matter. It's just not the best place in the world to be. If I didn't have to...If I wasn't getting paid to be here, I wouldn't be here, you know what I mean? It's not that ...There's no cable. There's no...There's just no freedom. There's really no freedom for staff. I can't just get up and leave. And the residents have it worse than us. They can't get up off their seat and move, you know?"

Juvenile-program workers, then, sometimes also saw themselves as playing a version of the Game of Outlaw in the facility. When the point system fails to regulate young people's behavior, juvenile-program workers fall back on the use of force. Most of these workers are large, muscular men. While some young people complain about the occasional brutality of the workers, the use of force commands status in the Game of Outlaw and the Game of Law. During an interview with Terrence, we were temporarily interrupted by a staff member whom I would later interview. The interaction suggests that the rules of the Game of Outlaw sometimes become part of the repertoire used by staff as well:

Terrence: People act up for no reason in here. Like you be chillin', whatever, and then they just gonna be loud and go against the rules for no reason at all, it's just stupid, stupidity, know what I'm sayin'.
[Juvenile-Program Worker enters the unit.]
Juvenile-Program Worker: Snitch.
Terrence: Who was that? There's no reason for that, so…What was that about? What the hell you talking about? [Laugh]

It was unclear whether the juvenile-program worker was accusing Terrence of snitching on other residents or snitching on staff. Nevertheless, this exchange suggests that the code of loyalty is understood by staff and is perhaps used to keep incidents from being reported. This expectation of loyalty between staff and residents was made even clearer in another account:

Interviewer: In instances of physical contact between you and the staff, do you think appropriate force has been used?
Resident: No. Because I told my mother this one staff member, he hit me…

Interviewer: Why did he hit you?
Resident: Because I was askin' why my points always bad. I don't even do nothing in the unit to get my points taken. He

said, "Kid, you're a retard. I don't like you and I'm gonna keep takin' your points." That's the exact words he told me. I told my mother, and my mother told the unit manager. Then the staff got back to me and they thought I snitched. So now in the unit, everyone calls me that. I get harassed every day. The staff, like if you say they're hittin' you, there's nothing you can do about it. You'll just get hit more.

Interviewer: Do you get hit here?
Resident: Oh yeah.

Interviewer: By who?
Resident: Staff.

Interviewer: When do they hit you?
Resident: When I told on that dude, when I asked him about my points, when he smacked me. The next day, I got confronted by another staff that was friends with him. That wasn't good at all.

Accounts of such staff violence were very rare in the interviews I conducted. Nevertheless, this account shows how staff adopted the rules of the Game of Outlaw to their own advantage, turning a resident into a "snitch" among his peers even when he was reporting abuse by staff. The Game of Law has a brutal underbelly not far from the rules of the Game of Outlaw.

The Game of Law that young men must negotiate in the Training School is not, then, a unified or comprehensive constellation of practices and is certainly not the Foucaultian panopticon through which disciplined subjects are constructed. The Game of Law is, rather, a somewhat loose set of criteria for behavior that reflect—in turn—the managerial needs of juvenile-program workers and the only partially articulated assumptions of administrators and staff about what constitutes a "good man."

The extent of *disorganization* actually makes space for more radical programming in the facility. The Broad Street Studio was an arts organization for at-risk youth in Providence and began providing regular workshops at the Training School beginning in 2000. As *Hidden TREWTH* became more established at the Training School, it became one of Broad Street Studio's regularly scheduled weekly workshops. Yet Sam Seidel, then the director of Broad Street Studio, unambiguously criticized the point system by which the rest of the facility organized itself:

> When you're not instilling a desire to hear what's going on, you're only telling somebody they can't talk 'cause they'll lose points.... It works with some kids and then other kids either are genuinely unafraid and just don't care and are unafraid, or [they] feel the need to show that they're tough. And then it almost goes out the window and it's almost an incentive to act up because people need to show that they're tough. Or for some people, the only thing they feel confident they can do is get in the most trouble out of anybody. So you put a bunch of people who, like, that's the only thing they've ever been recognized for in a room together and it can just get really out of control.

Broad Street Studio teaching staff, of which there were at least ten members, were required to fill out detailed evaluations of resident behavior after each arts workshop. Misbehavior could be grounds for discounting points. Yet no Broad Street Studio staff member, as far as I knew, ever gave any resident anything less than a perfect score, undermining the evaluation's usefulness. That a constituency in the Training School could so universally reject the disciplinary principles on which the Game of Law is based further highlights this game's vulnerability.

THE GAME OF LAW AND ITS LIMITS

Staff and administration at the Rhode Island Training School set the framework for a new game that many young offenders play. Like the shop floor game in Burawoy's well-known study (1979), the Game of Law offers enough uncertainty for many young people to feel invested in these new standards for behavior. In working to achieve points and to gain new privileges, young men enact an insider masculinity suitable for a life of low-wage work. The most successful of these young men are incorporated into the clerical staff of the facility, a special privilege that allows them a degree of freedom from the scrutiny of juvenile-program workers, while at the same time they become subject to the clock.

Despite the simplicity of the point system, a degree of disorganization and contradiction permeates the operation of the facility. Teachers and line staff seem unconvinced about the facility's rehabilitative potential, conflating the goals of treatment with those of facility management and disagreeing even among themselves about what the ends of the Game of Law should be. The young men who play the Game of Law, then, focus much more on their own acquisition of points and levels than they do on the game's underlying purpose, which many residents and staff at the facility seemed hard-pressed to explain.

However, whether or not young men choose to play the Game of Law and work to achieve behavioral points, every young man in the facility must somehow make sense of the stringent rules and close supervision they confront at the facility. The variety of ways in which they do so is where I now turn.

CHAPTER FOUR

Adapting to the Game of Law

Martin, a tall white resident with a loping stride, was one of the most enthusiastic participants in our first *Hidden TREWTH* workshops. As I left after my first day, he took me aside and told me that he had been praying for a program like this. Yet Martin seemed enthusiastic about almost every program to arrive at the gates of the Training School. Having met "Pastor Mike," a minister who led Bible studies for residents at the facility, Martin had been a quick convert. His behavior at the facility had been impeccable ever since, and he was quickly elevated to what might be considered the crowning achievement of young men involved in the Game of Law: administrative assistant to the principal. During most of my early visits to the facility, Martin was stationed at a small desk kitty-corner to the principal's secretary, copying, collating, and otherwise helping out. He had more physical freedom and more independence than any other resident. I often thought he could have walked out the front gates without anyone noticing.

Martin became a sort of poster boy for the conversion to religious faith within the Training School. He published a book of his religious poetry in which he linked his own salvation to religious revelation, and he was permitted to leave the facility in order to attend a Martin Luther King Jr. awards ceremony at a local school. A few weeks before his release, rumors circulated that he had assaulted another resident. But the story of his redemption was so deeply ingrained in everyone's imagination that this infraction was not enough to undermine it. Martin was released on time.

As mentioned in chapter 3, Martin was the only released resident I interviewed whom staff remembered as a "success." After his release, faith led him away from crime and straight into marriage with a woman he did not know well. Remembering his two closest friends at the Training School, Martin says, "Them dudes kind of kept me, kind of kept my mind absorbed still in the game, still on the street lingo. But they also affected my life somewhat." Martin's separation from the Game of Outlaw had to be pure, and complete.

Almost a year after our interview, Martin called me up in the middle of the afternoon requesting a ride to pick up his paycheck that evening from a big box store where he had been working as a cashier. We had not talked intimately since the interview, and I was interested in what he was now up to. It turned out to be an eighty-minute drive in each direction. And it turned out to be pouring rain by the time we met up.

Martin was eager to tell me about his faith. He spoke of the community he had found in his church in Barrington—how he was learning Portuguese and teaching a woman English, how there were people from twenty-three countries in the church, and how they welcomed him from the Training School with balloons and celebration. As the conversation proceeded, Martin also told me that there was only one true God—that believers in other faiths and nonbelievers were condemned to hell. He pointed to the sins of Jews to explain the current violence in Israel, asserted that sickness was a product of sin. He asked me about theories of evolution and laughed at my limited explanation.

Eventually, the conversation came around to the question of crime and the question of evil in the world. Martin asked, "What about murderers, Adam, what about rapists, what would you say about them?" I began discussing some of the structural reasons I thought young men were involved in crime—lack of jobs, poor schools, problems in young people's families, the relative glamour of the drug trade. Martin began to agree with me and then quickly turned inward, putting his hand to his head and closing his eyes. Over and over again, swaying, he repeated "I don't agree, I don't agree, I don't agree." Eventually he formulated his argument: "Look at me! My parents were both crack heads, I was abused, and look where I'm at! I can't believe what you're saying." He had a point. His own life was in many ways a testament to the power of individual will in the face of overwhelming odds. But his emphasis on personal responsibility, and on a Manichean world of good and evil, masked his own still very limited horizons. Martin's efforts to distinguish himself from his former friends at the Training School seemed to erase or at least diminish his critique of the forces that drove him to low-wage work.

While the *pure critique* outlined in chapter 2 reproduces criminality, Martin seemed to have assumed a *pure idealism*, a dogmatic belief in individual responsibility and rigid separation between good and evil that sustained him while disconnecting him entirely from the life he had left behind.

THE POSSIBILITIES AND PERILS
OF THE GAME OF LAW

Perhaps in part because the Game of Law offers so little in the way of what young people should do, and so much in the way of what they should refrain from doing, those young people who adhere to the Game of Law most strictly seem likely to develop a pure idealism that helps them sustain their commitment to a lifestyle that otherwise provides so little.

Investment in the Game of Law, and the elaboration of pure idealism, seemed most likely to occur among those young men less invested in the Game of Outlaw—more likely to occur among working-class young men than young men in deep poverty, and more likely to occur among white young men than young men of color. Martin's case was exceptional in the extent to which he was offered positive feedback for his conversion and had a community to reinforce his newfound belief on the outside.

Some residents recognized the difficulty of believing in their own transformations from a position of incarceration. Paradoxically, while putting forward an understanding of masculinity based on self-control and individual responsibility, staff of the Training School themselves depend on an elaborate *social* system of rewards and sanctions to foster this individualism, a system of rewards absent from life on the outside. Many young men considering the Game of Law seemed to recognize the tensions between playing the Game of Law on the inside and staying out upon release:

Resident: Well, I'm going through change now but I can't really see the change or feel the change till I leave here because there's nothing I can do when I'm here. Like, I don't swear, before when I was out I used to swear a storm. People used to look at me differently cause I was swearin' all the time. But I learned to control my swearin' and my negative attitudes....It's harder when you come out of here, going back to the same, the same world. It's not...the streets where the same people are. Cause when you're here, you think everything's changing, but on the streets nothing's changing. Everything's the same. I always think it's gonna be different every time I get out of a place like this or any other place I thought it'd be different but it's always the same....

Interviewer: Tell me some things you've learned at the Training School.

Resident: I don't know if I have. They sent me to anger management or something like that...and I passed and everything, but we still have to see if that stuff worked on me. I doubt it, really.... Interviewer: If you were to design the ideal program for young people getting out of the RITS, what would it look like? What effects would it have?
Resident: See, the way I see it, this place doesn't really work because...you know, I mean, they control us here, right? Tell us what to do, how to do it, when to do it...we got all that control, so we don't really learn how to...like, I mean, how to keep in check on our own...some people learn, but that's on they own 'cause they want to, not because of what they teach us here...Well, my point is that getting out of this place, they gotta help us to...I mean, change circumstances.

Like we get out and still got no money, say...then we go back to our neighborhood, same people, same old shit, right?

Even those young men willing to consider the game put forward by the Training School, then, were skeptical of their own transformations. They seemed to recognize that the Training School provides specific social circumstances in which a notion of individual responsibility is possible, while the social world outside presents different pressures.

THE UNIVERSITY OF CRANSTON

But if the Game of Law does not provide young men with a coherent way of understanding themselves, it does provide a huge amount of resources for young men who are incarcerated. A Broad Street Studio colleague of mine would often joke that the only thing wrong with the Training School was the walls around it. Open it up, he said, and young men would come flocking to it, given the resources inside. When speaking about his work there, this man refers to the facility as the University of Cranston, Cranston being the town in which the Training School is located.

One of the most fundamental dictates of criminal justice practice throughout modern history has been the principle of *less eligibility*, or the idea that a punishment must not be preferable to life in the absence of that punishment. Paradoxically, however, if the Game of Law in large part serves the managerial dictates of the Training School, it also demands resources to which many young men do not regularly have access on the outside, such as relatively safe classrooms with small class sizes, an in-house medical clinic, and three meals a day. Legal challenges have prevented conditions of confinement in Rhode Island from declining to the levels at which they have been observed in some states. Many young people discussed going to the dentist for the first time in years during their time at the Training School. In 2004, the medical clinic in the facility discovered that a resident had a brain tumor and sent the resident to a local hospital for emergency surgery, likely saving his life. Compared with an already expensive thirty thousand dollars to maintain an adult in prison in Rhode Island for a year, it costs around a hundred thousand dollars per year to maintain a juvenile at the Rhode Island Training School.

Many staff members expressed discomfort at the extent of the resources provided. These staff members seemed concerned that the Training School did not serve as adequate deterrent, given the conditions of young people's lives on the outside. One juvenile-program worker stated, "If you're gonna make sure that I'm protected, I'm sheltered, I get food, I celebrate, you know, holidays and stuff here, and I don't get this outside, why leave? Why not come back, you know what I mean? ... If you're giving me everything, if I come to you needing something and you give it to me, and I come to you again needing something and you give it to me, why cut that off? Why cut that pipeline off?"

One teacher also acknowledged, "I mean the kid here is at least getting three meals that they don't have on the outside. And the kid knows. It's like, at least while I'm here I know that I can have my three meals. I still get the state soap, but at least I get soap to wash myself with. So it is hard."

The Training School meets basic needs that might go unmet on the outside, this teacher suggested. Young people sometimes get into situations, she continued, where taking advantage of the prison as a resource makes sense for the sake of the family: "Sometimes you have moms who are working two or three jobs because they're not home to watch the kids. And that's when they get into trouble because they're trying to get money because dad might be in prison or dead or gone, no money, no child support—deadbeat dads. So yeah, you know, coming here makes perfect sense. They don't get to see their family, but they also know they're not a burden anymore on their family, so to speak."

A head administrator, recognizing that young people likely do not choose incarceration, still acknowledged that a supportive Training School may fail to provide strong disincentives when compared to a life on the outside: "And for them, being through the Training School may not have been the worst experience of their lives because it's very supportive here. It may have been in fact a fairly decent experience. So if they're caught again, having made a lot of money and enjoyed themselves, then just having to come back here isn't a big deterrent." However reluctantly, then, the Training School seems to subvert the dogma of less eligibility, at least in certain respects, creating some unexpected opportunities for young men on the inside.

Many residents acknowledged the resources and opportunities that the Training School made available. James spoke in general about the school being the best part of his time at the facility, "And I'd like to say that the school in here is run well, I'm not gonna say any names who runs it, but that's like the best thing I look forward to every day is goin' to school, and when we're on vacation it kinda sucks. But, that's like the only good thing about this place is the schooling, because you're not in your room and you're learning stuff. So that's what I look forward to every day is going to schooling."

Anthony also described how his experience in school at the Training School let him feel a sense of redemption, having been kicked out of many of the schools in Providence: "Turning point for the positive would have to be getting my GED. 'Cause I just got kicked out of Providence school system and they told me that I couldn't go back. So that made me realize that even without their help, whatever you want to do can still be done. Whether they tell you you can do it or not, it doesn't really apply, 'cause you don't have to listen to anybody."

Anthony's experience giving a graduation speech at the Training School was also a significant milestone for him, both in terms of the development of his public-speaking skills and in terms of feeling rewarded and recognized for something outside of his participation in the Game of Outlaw: "[The graduation speech] was actually my first time public speaking, in front of probably about three hundred people, some judges, my family, bunch of other people's families, a bunch of kids I was in the Training School with. I was kind of nervous at first, but then it was just like, 'I wrote it, whether they like it or not, oh well. Shit happens, you can't please everybody.' That actually helped me get out early too."

Harmony emphasized the advantages of juvenile prison more basically: "You might not have food on the outside, and then you have food, all three meals a day in jail. Jail's not all that bad. Everyone talks about the bad parts of jail, but jail does have its good parts." Nick, a resident with a history of mental illness, described how he found support inside the Training School that was unavailable on the outside:

Um, what I'd miss out of being here? Talking to people. I mean, I'll still talk to people out there, but in here you get to talk to a lot of people. You talk to social workers, the case manager, people in the school building. You get to do a lot of programs. Out there there's not programs for you. Once you're out there you have little things. For the work that you do, I mean, I could probably do it, but I don't know, you probably have to get accepted for that. Let's see, what else I'd miss? Not feeling alone. When you're here, you don't feel alone. But when I'm out there, I feel like I have pretty much no one.

For those young men who have dropped out of bad school systems before arrest, or who have not been able to rely on three meals a day, or who are in desperate need of mental-health services, the Training School actually serves as an important educational institution and social-service agency.

THE TRAINING SCHOOL AND THE GAME OF OUTLAW

That being said, many young men at the Training School merely reproduce the Game of Outlaw inside the facility. Allen, a young black man in maximum security, wore his family's criminal history as a badge. Asked who he looked up to, he replied without hesitation: "My father. My dad's a G [a gangster]. Allen J———. Everybody wants to be a G. But he's an actual real gangster. I want to be like him. I'm a G, but he's a G G." His father, mother, aunt, and uncles had all been in and out of prison, but he asserted that this secondhand experience with incarceration "don't got shit to do with me [being] locked up."

Describing other residents' perceptions of him within the Training School, he explained how the expression of violence in the facility is necessary to preserve status, "Some people show me love, some people hate me, all respect me. Because they know I don't care...I had to show that two weeks ago...Stung that nigga shit [slaps hand]. I haven't banged on someone in a while, getting soft. I had to let him know not to let him run his mouth. Not me."

Since he had not "banged on someone in a while," Allen was worried that he had begun to look weak among other Training School residents. While the proximate cause of his assault was someone "running his mouth," Allen admitted that the more general purpose of the attack was to show others he did not care about the consequences of his violence.

One's position in the Game of Outlaw is not rendered insignificant by the Game of Law. Indeed, for many young men the Training School is just another arena in which to play the Game of Outlaw. While these young men are forced to navigate the Game of Law given its prevalence in the facility, they dismiss it as another form of the police system against which to resist. The Training School becomes a place in which to enhance one's status and to enhance one's ability to play the Game of Outlaw outside. And given the holes left open by the Game of Law, the rules of the Game of Outlaw make their way into the daily interactions of young people in the facility as well.

In this way, the Training School is merely a reconfiguration of the Game of Outlaw on slightly different terrain. To the extent that the disciplinary regime of the juvenile prison is not total, the rules of the Game of Outlaw again become salient. The absence of a rigid treatment philosophy and program, discussed in the last chapter, leaves space for young people to associate with one another with relative autonomy, at least during certain portions of the day. Programming cuts leave even more time when young people are kept in "common rooms," playing cards or watching television. This lack of discipline lets elements of the Game of Outlaw reappear on the inside, as Rudolfo recounted:

> You say the wrong thing to the wrong person you get into a
> fight, whatever, you can catch a charge, some more time,
> probation, get sent to the Y [maximum-security unit], just
> stupid shit, stupid stuff like that.... That's why this place is
> just a waste of time, it's not worth it. I mean, yeah, they
> want you to realize don't mess up, this and that, if you keep
> on you're going to wind up in the ACI [the adult prison]
> but still, maybe the ACI is not better than this but it's not
> as much bullshit as it is in this place, you know what
> I'm sayin'.

Rudolfo described the threat of fights within the facility, revealing Training School discipline to be far from total. These fights resemble fights on the outside, in that they often involve boundaries (by race or gang affiliation) that have salience on the outside as well. The extent to which one has a reputation for holding one's own in a fight serves as a disincentive for others to start trouble. Rudolfo suggested that the ACI may actually have "less bullshit," in that discipline may be tighter there.[1]

Young people's experiences in the Training School can also cement the oppositional relationship young people feel between themselves and persons of authority. The rules inside are even more arbitrary than the laws outside, the guards often more brutal than the police outside. Robert did not think the disciplinary system served any purpose at all:

Robert: I don't think they really want us to do anything besides get our level four. That's the only thing they seem to want us to do is get our level four.

Adam: What does that mean?
Robert: It doesn't mean nothing, that's the whole point. It don't mean nothing.

For Robert, the point system represented an arbitrary exercise of authority and seemed to betray the facility's lack of concern for the well-being of residents themselves. Several former residents also remembered chafing against what felt like an arbitrary rigidity on the part of the Training School. Anthony remembered it changing him for the worse:

Adam: Did being at the Training School change how you described yourself? Did it change you?
Anthony: Yes.

Adam: In what ways?
Anthony: It made me a lot more stubborn, and a lot more resistant to authority.

Adam: Why?
Anthony: Just because your day in the Training School is so regimented, you have to do this, this, this at these times every day. You start to get used to the schedule but at the same time, I hate authority, so I think, tend to think schedules and shit don't apply to me. Like I set my own schedule. Like, you tell me to get up at six-thirty in the morning every day, it's

like, why? For what? Where are we going? I'm still gonna
be locked up at the end of the day, why am I getting up
this early?

Harmony remembered feeling angry at the strict discipline in
the facility, which felt symbolic of the reasons she had become
involved in crime in the first place. Describing the disciplinary
regime, she recounted:

> Old-fashioned manners that we already know, we just ...
> They're trying to teach you probably some manners that
> you should have, like, in an extremely strict household. And
> I don't know how that's supposed to change anything.
> Because we act out probably because of those reasons as it
> is. So it doesn't really do nothing but condition us down to
> why we should hate them even more and why we should
> hate life even more.

Far from helping young people learn new ways of behaving,
Harmony suggested, the Training School's system of points and
levels only reinforced residents' aversion to arbitrary authority.
Young people would emerge from the facility more determined
to shake off the shackles of the state and live outside the boundaries of the law.

The Training School can also be seen as an organization in
which street smarts are augmented, in which young people learn
to play the game more adeptly. While the criminological literature recognizes how time in prison can enhance criminal commitments and introduce less serious offenders to more serious
offenders, young people emphasized the simple exchanges of
information that take place, as Luis observed, "I look at these
places like a school for criminals. Like every time you come in

here you just learn better things, and you just put them all together and you try to connect your mistakes with his mistakes and just try to make them better, or you try to, you try to, um, combine your knowledge with his knowledge, and then you just figure of a way you think is going to get you out of trouble."

Pushed on his definition of "out of trouble," Luis expanded:

From getting away, getting away from the cops. Like if you made a mistake by stayin' out there twenty-four-seven and the cops is seein' you. But you found a way, you're out there on the block sellin' every day the cops is seein' you, you come in here, you meet someone that's not out there every day but he's making money, say off a cell phone or something. The guy that was on the block, he's gonna make what he made as a mistake as not bein' seen by the cops, so he's gonna try to get a cell phone, and try not to be seen as much, but still keep his clientele, and still be out there sellin' and try to hide from the cops.

One resource to which all residents of the Training School have access is the collection of accounts of one another's failures (Sitkin 1992)—failures that provide (with every new arrival) updated records of police practices and what has not worked in terms of staying out. When shared, these failures (as well as previous strategic successes) help young people navigate life on the outside more adeptly.

THE SOAP ECONOMY AND AN INTRODUCTION TO INTERSECTING GAMES

The presence of the Game of Outlaw on the inside presents something of a paradox for many residents. For one to accept wholeheartedly the disciplinary mechanisms of the Training School, working toward attaining privileges within the facility, one must avoid fights—whether or not one is responsible for starting them. Yet without a certain street status in the facility, a resident is likely to be targeted, either for the scarce resources (candy, pens, etc.) he has or merely because the attack enhances the street status of another resident. This is only more likely if a resident is seen as truckling to prison administrators.

The opposite tension also exists, in that to win status in the Game of Outlaw one must also play by the rules of the Game of Law, at least to a certain extent. Without the adequate number of points to achieve a particular level, one still must go to bed earlier than other residents, is not allowed to listen to music, and is not given credit to spend on commodities at the canteen—all of which detract from one's street status.

In chapter 5 I examine how this tension makes possible a synthesis of these irreconcilable games that I call *critical practice*. Activities oriented toward one game to the exclusion of the other make success at *either* in some ways more difficult. Those who are able to succeed in either game are more likely to be adept at navigating both, treating each game more consciously as a game in order to be able fluidly to alternate games in different situations. Both games become mechanisms for achieving something beyond both.

In chapter 5, then, I discuss the reflective understandings of both games that emerge from this kind of synthesis. Here, I illustrate how these games come into tension through a description of the Training School's underground "soap economy." This economy—itself a product of the intersection of the Games of Law and Outlaw, might be understood as providing the practical incentives that make possible the critical practice examined in the next chapter.

According to several residents, soap acts as a kind of currency in the Training School. The exchange value of soap is significantly more valuable than its use value, meaning that "some people were just really really dirty and didn't give a fuck" so that they could hoard or exchange the soaps they were issued. Soap gives people "juice, pull."

Calvin, a white former resident, described the rather comprehensive exchange rate between different sorts of soaps and what sorts of soaps could be traded for different goods. State-issued soaps "weren't worth shit." Dial soaps were one step up from state soaps, but people still "looked at you as if you were funny" if you tried to exchange them. Irish Spring soaps were worth two dollars. And the Dove soaps were the most valuable. If you had white Dove bars "you were pimpin'," and if you had the pink bar you "were the fucking man." If you had the bar with the "blue dots on it" you were "God."

In terms of the soaps' value on the market, a state-issued soap would likely get you a couple of pictures from a pornographic magazine. The "really good" pictures were worth a couple of state-issued soaps. An Irish Spring soap would get you a magazine or a can of soda. A two-liter soda "probably ran somebody through a good three soaps, four soaps." You could even get a pair of Nike shoes if the price was right: probably something like twenty Irish Springs and forty Dove bars. That being said, the exchange rate was not an exact science, and how much you could get for your soaps "depended on how good you were of a hustler." Calvin explained, "Say somebody wanted a twenty-ounce bottle of Sprite, I'd be like okay, I got a twenty-ounce bottle of Sprite, give me a Dove for it. It all depends on your entrepreneurial skills. It's all that it really boils down to. How bad do you want it, and how much do I have. Supply and demand....Certain people can get more for their soap, certain people can get less. It's all about being able to talk and how slick you are."

The most straightforward way to accumulate soap was to buy it through the Training School's canteen. Points to spend at the canteen were correlated with behavioral points, in that those who had a higher disciplinary level were able to buy more. Moreover, in order to get away with accumulating soaps, a young man needed the silent complicity of the juvenile-program workers, or needed at least not to be suspected of hoarding soaps. Training School policy was that residents were allowed only two soaps in their cells, and staff room raids on residents suspected of smuggling were relatively frequent. A resident, then, had to be on good terms with staff in order to buy soaps legally and store them in his room.

On the other hand, many of the mechanisms through which people accumulated soaps resembled practices from the Game of Outlaw. Calvin remembered how he won soaps:

Adam: How did you get more soaps?
Calvin: How did I get more soap? Cards.

Adam: Cards?
Calvin: Yeah. Spades was a very popular game. You get to gamble. You're not supposed to gamble, but soaps are on the line every once in a while. And I lost a couple soaps, but it was worth it.

Stealing and robbing soaps from one another was also not unusual. In the middle of my interview with Allen, he got distracted by his plans for later that afternoon, "I got to come back [to the unit after lunch] and rob a Dove. 'Cause I'm trying to buy a walkman.... Doves is like dollars in here. I only got two left and that needs to last me. You can get everything—cigarettes, everything. Doves will get you anything."

According to Calvin, this practice of people "run[ning] into people's room to snatch up their soap" was fairly common. Those people who constantly traded their soap were treated like "custies," or drug buyers, always willing to sacrifice the little currency they had for something they could buy on the market.

The soap economy, then, was a hybrid between the Game of Outlaw and the Game of Law. To accumulate soaps was against Training School policy, yet one could not accumulate soap without a good relationship with line staff. The mechanisms through which young men accumulated soap mirrored the practices of the Game of Outlaw, yet a young man had to play the Game of Law in order to keep the soap he won.

The soap economy was a creative solution to the limitations imposed on young people within the Training School. The restrictions on young men from both the Game of Law and the Game of Outlaw made necessary a kind of resourcefulness that many had not recognized in themselves before. As Calvin remembered, "Because in there you don't have monetary units, you don't have any money, so you work with what you have. I mean, in that sense that was a positive. I guess you could say, a positive experience or positive lesson, is how to become resourceful with what you have." This alternative economy serves as a useful introduction to the political possibilities embedded in the intersection between the Game of Outlaw and the Game of Law.

PART III

Critical Practice

The bus lines in Rhode Island work fine for the spring and summer, when you can walk a few blocks without the chill getting into your blood. From November to February, though, if you can find a ride—any ride—you take it.

That's how Harmony wound up in my car with Laura and me on our way back to downtown Providence from a Training School performance in late 2001. She had been released from the women's facility, half a mile down a dirt road from the Training School, only a week or so before the show but had been permitted to return to the facility to perform a piece. It was our first time meeting her, but that didn't seem to stop her from laying down everything she had learned during her last time incarcerated. For a white seventeen-year-old from Pawtucket—an old mill town adjacent to Providence—Harmony knew an awful lot about Malcolm X, Huey Newton, and the Black Panther Party.

Harmony and Anthony had been dating since before their last Training School detentions and in so doing had managed to transcend many of the categories that have salience for the young people with whom I worked: geography, race, gang affiliation. Harmony had been a member of the Bloods gang whereas Anthony was part of the Folk Nation. Their unlikely partnership had not made them abandon their respective affiliations but had caused each of them to be more flexible about whom they'd call friends.

Harmony got out at the same time Jacob was killed, almost to the day. It seemed to me a small miracle, since Harmony was one of the only people who could get through to Anthony as he struggled with the loss of his best friend. Harmony was not only an emotional partner to Anthony but was also one of the few young people who could articulate exactly what Anthony had to lose by returning to the Game of Outlaw.

Their partnership seemed to me to keep both of them out of crime, but that wasn't exactly how their mothers saw it. Anthony and Harmony had been arrested in a stolen car together before their last Training School bids. Harmony's mother especially wanted her to have nothing to do with Anthony, and nothing to do with Providence. She would rather Harmony stayed in the relative quiet of Pawtucket, despite the fact that many of Harmony's old gang associates were themselves Pawtucket residents.

It was freezing and snowy and only a few days from Christmas, then, when Harmony called me from the pay phone of a 7-Eleven parking lot a couple of blocks from her mother's house. She and Anthony were together, and Harmony's mother wouldn't let them in the house. Without thinking twice I drove out to pick them up and welcomed them to stay the night in my apartment. They would stay there for the next couple of weeks, ordering disgusting five-dollar pizzas from the corner pizza parlor, writing poetry, and having more sex than Anthony could handle. They made this public as I returned home from work the day after they had arrived. Harmony was joking with Anthony about his inability to "put out," and Anthony was laughing sheepishly.

As I took off for my parents' house for Christmas, I thought of my apartment as a kind of sanctuary for the two of them. The apartment was in an abandoned downtown space, unmarked territory for any gang, and close to AS220, the organization at which we all worked. But even then, the world's expectations were hard to keep at bay. When I called to check in, Anthony reported that my landlord—the owner of the clothing store below—had been asking for me nervously. Anthony had told him that he was apartment sitting while I was away for the holidays, but this hadn't seemed to help. After a week, the landlord started calling my name up to the apartment from the street below. Anthony and I joked that the landlord must have thought I had been bound and gagged. When I got back to the apartment, I came in unannounced and pretended to be the landlord, calling my name as Anthony had told me the landlord had done. Anthony came out of one of the bedrooms ready for a fight, and we all had a good laugh about it for weeks.

Anthony described his own previous participation in crime as "just another illegal life." Like many other young men deeply invested in the Game of Outlaw, he seemed to see crime as indistinguishable from legal work. Yet Anthony was critical of the Game of Outlaw as well:

'Kay, from like, just watching everything I seen growing up, people hustling, everyone in a rush to get something accomplished but no one really sure what. Drug dealers a perfect example. Like, they hustle all day just to get money. At the end of the day all they do with their money is buy more drugs, or buy clothes and shit that doesn't really matter. But they go out and just look, so they can look better in front of the next person on the block who they really don't care about. And it's the same thing in any form of life. Like a doctor works seventy hours a week to buy a brand new Mercedes to impress people he doesn't even

know. Probably doesn't want the car, but because he's a
doctor, and because he makes a certain amount of money a
year he has to have that status symbol, to appear successful,
regardless of how happy he is.

Anthony saw similarities between the drug dealer and the
doctor—how they each work to make money but each make
money only in order to prove their status in relationship to
others. He saw both lives as being driven by forces outside of
their control, both the drug dealer and the doctor as trying to
achieve a kind of status without regard for "how happy" they
are. This critique was different from the pure critique I observed
among young men invested in crime, whose exclusion from
productive work allows them trenchant but unreflective observations that serve to reproduce their own criminality and
exclusion. Anthony seemed instead to recognize the unreflec-
tiveness of both games and sought to live in a way that transcended both.

What struck me initially about Anthony's and Harmony's
critiques of the Game of Outlaw was their lack of guilt or regret
about participation in crime.[1] Like Anthony, Harmony had no
moral qualm with young people's involvement in crime. Rather,
she seemed to understand crime as a careless and ineffective
rebellion against an oppressive society. Her understanding of the
Training School was that it just reinforces this rebellion:

[In the Training School] we're being told to be the way that
we've been rebelling against our whole lives because shit's
fucked up. Because they won't give certain people jobs
'cause the way they look or you can't do this or teachers
don't care. You know what I mean? Things like that. Shit's

fucked up at home. You can't pay attention to work like
that, to schoolwork. You're worried about getting a job and
buying shit for yourself because you don't have shit to go to
school with. You don't have paper. You don't have pens.
You get in trouble when you go to school because you don't
have those things. You don't have a backpack. Things like
that, it fucks you up, you know.

But for Harmony, playing the Game of Outlaw meant
being "caught" in a society toward which she felt a certain
amount of disgust: "I just don't want to be a part of society,
basically. Because I don't like it, and I'm trying to help
people who are oppressed within it." She articulated her
political philosophy:

> Anybody can have a gun. Anybody can kill anybody. That
> doesn't make you superior or stronger than anybody else
> because you can do that, because you can fire a gun. And I
> never really thought like that anyway, but I realized that if
> I'm gonna live my life right, I need to live without all that
> stuff. And if somebody's gonna try an' kill me, then some-
> body's gonna kill me because I'm not gonna sit there and
> stoop to that level. Because I feel that that's stooping to a
> level that the government—not necessarily wants me—but
> there's so many traps and so many things out there, you
> know what I mean? I'm not gonna fall into none of those
> things 'cause I'm not gonna let anybody win.

She challenged the idea that having a gun makes someone
tough and reinterpreted the violence of the Game of Outlaw as
"stooping to a level" that the state actually supports, in that it
allows the state to regulate and repress young people: "I just
know if I fall into their trap, then they win, and if I go sit there

and sell drugs and go get stubborn and say 'fuck a regular job'....If you say that, then that's what they want you to do.... They want to see you fuck up, they want to see you mess up. You just gotta stay positive."

The possibility for this sort of understanding emerged from the tension between the Game of Law and the Game of Outlaw in the Training School. Those most successful in the facility, according to either the standards of the Game of Law or the standards of the Game of Outlaw, are those who learn to "code switch" (Delpit 1995), who learn to walk the line between the rules of the Game of Law and the rules of the Game of Outlaw. Sam Seidel, the director of Broad Street Studio at the time I interviewed him, used education scholar Lisa Delpit's term when I asked him what he thinks it takes for young people to stay out of prison upon release: "I like to think a lot of it is about code switching—being willing to dress up a little and talk in a way that might not be who you are, but at least at first, opening up relationships, getting your foot in the door, making people feel comfortable with you."

This code switching—a self-conscious relationship to each game as a game—seems to facilitate reflection about both of the games within which one is engaged and makes possible a sort of creativity that cannot emerge through participation in one game alone.

CRITICAL PRACTICE AND MASCULINITY

Critical practice is a second-order understanding of both games, an ability to see each game as a "hustle" while not letting either dictate one's activity unconsciously. The goals of young men engaging in critical practice are no longer unrecognized aspirations for masculinity. Rather, young men engaged in critical practice seem to explore what it would mean to posit their own goals self-consciously.

In both the Game of Outlaw and the Game of Law, women seem little more than commodities to be acquired, consumed, or protected. The forms of this objectification differ, of course, as the sexual consumption of the Game of Outlaw gives way to the protective paternalism of the Game of Law. Yet it is only in critical practice, it seems, that young men recognize women's subjectivity. Young men and young women are able more fully to be partners in reimagining the social world that restricts them both.

In a book about masculinity, Harmony's case as a young woman deserves special attention.[2] Understanding masculinity as a set of practices (as opposed to an identity) makes it easier to conceive of women acting "masculine." But understanding Harmony as masculine seems an oversimplification. On the one hand, when I first met her, Harmony almost always wore baggy jeans, sports jerseys, and kept her long hair pulled back and out of the way. She wore almost no makeup and no jewelry. As a performance artist, she exuded the same kind of aggressive self-assertion I had come to associate with outsider masculinity, and she walked with the same swagger as many of the young men with whom I worked. As explored in chapter 2, Harmony had also been deeply embedded in the Game of Outlaw, having gotten involved in selling drugs through her own brother and having felt the particular kind of power that she could have through gang involvement.[3]

Yet in other ways it seemed Harmony had always been an outsider to the Game of Outlaw. When I was getting to know her, Harmony still felt some connection to her Pawtucket gang, yet she seemed often to be in a position of offering emotional support to the others in her set. As soon as she began working with me at the Training School, the young men in our workshops seemed to treat her with a kind of respect that I couldn't quite place. She combined a deep understanding of the Game of Outlaw with a kind of caring and counseling that was in short supply among other young men, bridging the roles of friend, sister, and mentor.[4]

By the time I met her, Harmony was using this insider/outsider status to become one of the most powerful voices on behalf of critical practice, working with young men to institutionalize a space in which they could reflect on the conditions that had driven them to crime. Although all of the young men released from the Training School were barred from returning to the facility, Harmony was permitted to join us in our workshops, where she quickly became a kind of symbol for what many young men wanted to become. Far from the sexualized nature of the male-female interactions in our early *Hidden TREWTH* workshops, Harmony would sit in the corner each week with a mentee, patiently educating him on the *true* nature of the Game of Outlaw.

Critical practice seems to be a movement toward degendered practice, in that the categories of masculinity and femininity lose some of their importance. At the level of interaction, young men and young women worked collaboratively in a way I hadn't seen before. Furthermore, they reflected on and sought to change the broader structural arrangements of power that constricted *both* women *and* these marginalized young men. What seems especially remarkable about critical practice is the way that it combines change at the level of young men and young women's interpersonal interaction *and* change at the more structural level. This is significant in light of critiques of men's antisexist work and of feminist work that privileges women's "way of seeing the world" (Lorber 2005: 139), critiques that suggest that these forms of resistance might unintentionally reify gender categories at the same time they challenge existing distributions of institutional power.[5] For the young people I study it was only in the context of contesting broader arrangements of power that more degendered ways of interacting seemed to become more possible.

CHAPTER FIVE

The *Hidden TREWTH* and the Possibility of Critical Practice

> The *Hidden TREWTH*... is a newspaper based on the realness of the world today.... We the residents of the Training School will be heard. We aren't going to hide the fact that the system is corrupted. We won't give up without a fight. We will make it through the strife that they put us through because we are not weak.
>
> —Richard, introduction to *Hidden TREWTH*, nos. 7/8 (July 2002–November 2002)

The earliest issues of *Hidden TREWTH* didn't receive much attention from the Training School staff or administration. Maybe they didn't read it. Or maybe they assumed that, given many programs' short runs at the facility, *Hidden TREWTH* wasn't worth complaining about. Some of residents' boldest critiques of the juvenile correctional system and most profane language, then, were met with silence.

This silence broke during our fourth issue, in January of 2002. Under a pseudonym, Richard had written a very short and simple piece titled, "Why," in which he asked, "Why do we get treated like we do while we're in here? Staff expect us to respect them, but they don't respect us. It goes both ways. In order to get respect you gotta give it." Suddenly the paper was treated like an insurrection. We heard that one of the juvenile-program workers from maximum security had complained to the correctional officers' union, and pretty soon we were banned from conducting workshops in that part of the facility. The principal of the Training School, a longtime ally of ours, began to censor the content of the newspaper more stringently based on criteria we did not understand. Residents were outraged. Some stopped wanting to write for the paper at all.

Over the course of a year, however, Laura helped to turn young men's despondency into a productive conversation about the politics of an organization like the Training School. She brought in the writing of Antonio Gramsci and introduced him as a political prisoner who had had to write his theory in code in order to avoid censorship (or worse) from the Italian fascist authorities. Young men began to experiment with ways of expressing themselves that would convey their message without setting off the alarm bells of administrators.

In our workshops, we began strategizing about how to continue with the paper's operation. Eventually, thanks to the leadership of a couple of administrators as well as Laura's work with residents, we reached agreement about a process for publication that was explained in the May–June 2003 issue:

> For the first time ever, the writing published in Hidden TREWTH was approved through a process involving a group of people working as a collective to come to decisions.... The group, made of adults and youth; [Training

School] staff members and residents; AS220 class participants and group facilitators, read all of the pieces together
and discussed them. Decisions about what is appropriate to
be published regarding pieces that spoke of violence and
some other controversial subjects were driven by whether
the group could hear the writer struggling to make his/her
way to a more positive state of mind. The overall message
communicated by the piece is more important than specifics
of the language used.

—*Hidden TREWTH*, no. 11 (May–June 2003)

Of course, this compromise did not end tensions in the relationship between Broad Street Studio (which sponsored the
paper) and the Training School, which to this day sometimes
still reach breaking point. At the end of every workshop series,
the studio put on a "showcase" of artwork, music, and writing
for other residents in the school cafeteria. As the administration
began tightening its supervision of *Hidden TREWTH*, it also
began to examine everything that would be said or displayed at
the showcase. Yet young men still occasionally tested the boundaries. During one especially memorable incident, a young man
began insulting staff before the principal turned off his micro-
phone. During another showcase, a resident performed
a Spanish rap that hadn't been approved and was disciplined
after his words inspired the audience to bang in unison on the
cafeteria tables.

Still, Broad Street Studio—with the work and voices of the
young men who make up its workshops leading the way—has
managed to win and sustain a voice at the Training School. As
Broad Street Studio grew, young people involved in the studio's
programming began to take on staff roles as well, adding to the

number of staff who had the most intimate knowledge of the neighborhoods in which young people were living. Staff members were able to draw on diverse repertoires in the ways they conceived of their work and the ways they went about solving organizational problems.

Critical practice is a reflection on both the Game of Law and the Game of Outlaw that allows young people to see, and act, beyond both. Instead of competing with one another over who can be the most masculine, young men begin to think collectively and strategically about how to live their lives and how to address their common challenges. Masculinity, which seems to serve as the always-present and yet rarely noticed lynchpin of both the Game of Outlaw and the Game of Law, loses its rigidity. Young men are able to imagine family and work lives that break open the rules of the games in which they have been unreflectively engaged.

In this chapter, I argue that it is the structural tension between the Game of Outlaw and the Game of Law that allows space for critical practice to emerge for young men in the Training School. The possibility for critical practice to emerge exists most powerfully for those most invested in the Game of Outlaw. These young men use the resources of the Training School to develop new knowledge and use the programming at the Training School to develop new social networks and new understandings. They come to reconceptualize the resources to which they have access and, even more fundamentally, the parts of themselves they most value. The relationships that they establish with certain staff members challenge their blanket critiques of authority, on the one hand, while the intimacy of the repression they face in the Training School reaffirms their commitment to fighting injustice, on the other. The relationships they form with other young people across the boundaries of race and neighborhood cement their understanding of young offenders as a "class" while rendering less powerful the factionalism that exists among young people in the street.

The creativity made possible by the diverse backgrounds and new perspectives on criminality offered by outsiders with certain types of political consciousness allow some young people to break out of their habitual involvement in criminality while in the Training School.[1] The particular degree of repression young people face in the Training School, powerful but incomplete, actually seems to make possible this political understanding.[2]

SPACE

The first and most basic condition necessary for the emergence of critical practice is the autonomy that the Training School has from the Game of Outlaw. As examined in previous chapters, this space does not necessarily produce critical practice. Some young men reincorporate the rules of the Game of Outlaw into the Game of Law and use the Training School to reinforce their status in the Game of Outlaw. Others try to abandon the Game of Outlaw altogether and adopt the rules and understandings of the Game of Law entirely. Still, the Training School does provide a world unlike that of the streets, a space of relative autonomy from the rules of the Game of Outlaw. Rudolfo said, "Just being here, 'cause they say, in jail you got time to think. And believe it or not you've got time to think 'cause all you have in here, you do wake up in the morning, go to school, do whatever you got to do, but it's not like you're going out on the set and doing what you got to do. In here you're just, you're locked up."

Frank went further, asserting that this time for reflection leads explicitly to the possibility of personal change: "You think about it and you start realizing this isn't what you want, and then when you start thinking about, 'Well, the reason I got here is because I'm always trying to prove to somebody and doing things that I probably wouldn't normally do, if I wasn't trying to prove myself.' So then you just start realizing that, and you, when you have time to think you start finding yourself and say, 'This really isn't me, and what is actually my character, and what situation should I actually be living?'"

Frank explained that his time in the facility had helped him find out who he really was. Harmony at least partly shared the opinion that the Training School was a necessary intervention in her life: "[Without the Training School] I woulda still been the same way because there's too much stuff going on around me [on the outside]. When you're in jail, the only thing you have to do is sit there and think."

Harmony went so far as to say that the emergence of critical practice was only possible in prison: "The best time to reach people is while they're incarcerated. Because when you're out, you don't care who's trying to talk to you about anything. I mean, I wouldn't have changed from who I was as a person to how I am with never going to jail. It woulda never happened. I woulda still been the same way because there's too much stuff going on around me."

The physical isolation and "space to think" does not by any means produce new understandings for young people in and of itself, any more than the philosopher, sitting alone in a darkened room, could discover the truth of the world. But since the Game of Outlaw and the understandings associated with it depend on actively *playing*, the physical isolation of the Training School at least makes these understandings less immediate and powerful.

BLING-BLING, BYE BYE

Critical practice seems associated with a rejection of the commodities on which the Game of Outlaw defines outsider masculinity. A divestment from material acquisition seems to make possible reflection on both the Game of Outlaw and on the Game of Law. This rejection is facilitated by the rules and regulations of the Training School, which make it impossible to be too invested in flashy commodities since there are strict limits on the goods that young people can possess within the facility. Rudolfo's "choice" to look "bummy and scrubby" (see the introduction) is revealing of the relative autonomy of the prison experience from the flashiness of the street.

Harmony explained how a desire for fashionable products left her "caught" in a society from which she wanted to distance herself:

> Well, I believe money is...I hate money. I wish there was no such thing as it. I think about that all the time. Having stuff is important. But I don't want to have stuff like that. Like I'm not...I used to worry about having twenty pairs of boots and having twenty pairs of sneakers and having seventy-five jerseys....Thousands of sweatpants and that. Now I just need enough to be alright, know what I mean? I'm not worried about it no more....It's important to me

having money in my pocket for food and being able to buy myself, you know, socks and whatever I need, you know, hair stuff, and you know, things I need to buy for myself to just live. But having money, money, money, like having mad chains and mad clothes for no apparent reason ... I'm not concerned with that. That's caught in society, you know, twisted thing.

Harmony saw "no apparent reason" for worrying about having lots of jewelry and clothing. As long as she had money for food, socks, and the occasional hair product—the things she needed "just to live"—she was fine. Anthony made the same point in my interview with him:

Adam: What do you need to live a fulfilling life?
Anthony: What do I need to lead a fulfilling life? Food, shelter, and family.

Adam: That's it?
Anthony: That's pretty much it. Like I don't need to have the brand-new pair of Tims on, but I like to so I do. I could survive, I could wear my old Tims and not have a problem with it. Like it wouldn't bother me how society perceives me, but, like the main things I need in my life are food, shelter, and family.

For both Anthony and Harmony, critical practice involved a renunciation of those consumer goods on which the Game of Outlaw was staked. A freedom from these needs, and a return to the essentials of "food, shelter, and family," seems to allow a perspective from which to critique both the Game of Law and the Game of Outlaw.

Even more fundamentally, however, those engaged in critical practice seem to care less about their status in relationship to others. Anthony said it "wouldn't bother [him]" how society perceived him if he didn't have the trappings of consumer culture. Rodney discussed the hypocrisy he saw in rich rap stars:

Rodney: To me, that's just trying to show off for everyone else. I feel that I don't have to show off for anyone else. Me, I'm just, I'm me, I'm Bear, I'm [Rodney]. Why be a commercial figure, you know?

Adam: How did you get that way of thinking?
Rodney:...How are you gonna be a rapper and be like, "Oh the poverty, the poverty," when you've been through it, but now you're making like...you have a nine-million, five-million dollar contract a year. So you're getting like five million dollars, that's for one-year of contract, you know what I mean? And then like you're still gonna talk about like rap poverty and all that? But yet you're not giving back. Come on, you probably don't need that whole million for the year, you know. But yet you're going out and buying your bling-bling, fancy cars. Your bank account, there's so many zeros on it with, like, large numbers is that like damn, like, you could support America. You and like five, six other rappers, singers, could support America. But you don't do it.

Rodney saw hypocrisy in rap stars' simultaneous critique of social injustice and their preoccupation with material wealth. He suggested that he did not have to "show off for anyone else," that he did not rely on a superiority to others to know who he was. The goods that had meaning for Rodney, then, were not those that displayed his ability to consume more than others but rather those that symbolized for him a link between himself and his history. A positional identity seemed to give way to a more reflective identity, in which Rodney saw himself as a historical subject, his own oppression linked to historical oppression of his ancestors:

> This choker that I'm wearing on my neck, it's like, it's real. And they only cost like thirty, fifty dollars. You know. And it actually has meaning to it. It's the colors of my tribe, you know. It's who I am. I'm half Indian, you know. Blackfoot, you know. Whatever happened to tradition? That's what makes me think of that. That's what made me think that I don't need all that. You know, 'cause once you go that route, you go commercial. And they'll tell you, "Oh, I'm real, I'm real. I'm a real ['cause] I'm a dawg. I'm a gansta." You know. Like, but look at your roots man, you know, don't come to me all, "The white man took over America…." Don't come at me with that if you're not gonna be traditional about it. You know, that's what makes me think that commercial, that all the money, it's just useless. 'Cause if they talking about that, then they hypocrites, 'cause they're not giving back to society. They're not giving back to the hood that they came from.

For Rodney, wearing clothing that represented his heritage was more important than outdoing other young men in terms of the money he spent. People engaged in critical practice seem to challenge the positional identity enacted through participation in the Game of Outlaw and the Game of Law.

COLLECTIVE CONSCIOUSNESS

At the same time that the Training School makes the bling-bling of the Game of Outlaw impossible, then, it also succeeds at challenging the social boundaries on which the Game of Outlaw is based. The relationships on which young people staked their identity reveal themselves as less meaningful than young people once assumed. And young people who have begun identifying with different gangs are instead brought into contact with one another, forced to befriend or at least to tolerate one another. The rare occasions on which gang conflict breaks out in the Training School pale in comparison with the ways in which young people—in their daily life at the facility—must work together collaboratively. By limiting the extent to which external (e.g., gang) divisions can appear inside, and by subjecting all young people to a similarly repressive regime, the physical environment of the Training School can help young people come to an awareness of similarities in their lives and positions.

Young people often feel abandoned by their peers on the inside. If outsider masculinity is enacted by young men among their peers, the limited loyalty of these peers—revealed for the first time—might help young men extract themselves from the Game of Outlaw. James expressed his realization of the limits of his peer group's friendship: "You really find out who your real friends are and who cares about you and who don't care about you. Because really all the people I used to hang around with, once you're gone for a while, they don't care about you no more. They forget about you. They don't send you...I could say I only got like two or three Christmas cards this year from people that I knew for a while and from my family, but no one else really cares about you."

Terrence, who had been incarcerated for more than one Christmas, discussed the process by which he realized the limited concern of his former friends:

> It's like, for the first three months you'll see letters, you'll
> see. Everybody, yeah, they got you, after a while it all fades,
> you know? It's like a mirage. I noticed that, it's a mirage.
> I'm thinking, "Yeah, yeah, yeah, they got me," there no
> letters comin' in no more. I'm askin' for real things, I'm
> like, "Yo, I might need a job when I get out." And every-
> thing's just hearsay. It's just words, it's just words, it's not
> really put into action. And that's why...when I get out, I do
> for myself. It could be from growing up, being raised not so
> much by my mother, but by my brothers, you know.

Harmony remembered the feeling of isolation and abandon-ment she experienced while incarcerated and how these feelings encouraged her to step out of the false sources of stability that led to her being locked up: "When you're in jail, you can't fall on none of those things 'cause nobody's there. Who's writing you? Probably one person that you knew, you know. Or your mother or you father, you know what I mean? You don't have those things to fall back on. And then you start to really realize what life's really about because those things were never really there for you like that because they're not there for you now, you know." The isolation of the Training School, these resi-dents suggested, is actually useful for getting some perspective on their own lives and on the limits of loyalty in the Game of Outlaw.

And while these previous relationships—formed through participation in the Game of Outlaw—become attenuated, young people's relationships with others in the Training School grow stronger. While this can just work to reinforce young people's commitment to criminality, it can also have the effect of opening young people's eyes to the arbitrariness of the social boundaries outside prison.

Asked if there was anything he missed about the Training School, Anthony described the unique sort of solidarity he experienced with young people in the Training School: "The whole group thing. That's like pretty much the reason people join sports teams, join class, group groups, activist groups, whatever, it's because you part of a group. Being in a unit with twenty people, or thirty, however many people are in your building. Being there, like as a group, that actually like, okay that's something that like you become accustomed to, and it's comforting knowing that everyone there is pretty much in the same situation you're in."

Anthony went on to describe the community of young people he developed while at the Training School, bonds forged by a common interest in writing about the injustices that they faced: "Another turning point was meeting [several residents named]. They got me, like we started flowin' a lot more, like that got me to take hip-hop a little more seriously, well as far as writing goes. And I started to worry about, it's not just what you write, but how you say it too, which really affects people a lot, cause a lot of trash MCs make a lot of money somehow."

These young people were from different neighborhoods in Providence, were involved in different peer groups on the outside. Inside the facility, however, they developed a common commitment to political writing, writing that "affects people." This peer group, in turn, was facilitated by classes run by the arts organization Broad Street Studio and by several young writing teachers committed to the development of this community.

RESOURCES AND RESOURCEFULNESS

Finally, as observed in chapter 4, the Training School offers access to educational and cultural resources to which young men do not, in their outside lives, have easy access. While many of the teachers in the Training School have a traditional social-service orientation to their work, some of the people interested in teaching and working at the facility are interested because of the political implications of work within a locked facility. Radical perspectives on crime and incarceration, then, actually make their way into some of the programming at the facility, offering young people new ways of thinking about their own involvement in crime.[3]

Critical practice was likely facilitated by these interventions from outsiders. Yet I would argue that these interventions were influential largely because of the structural conditions in which they took place. Countless *other* organizers, intellectuals, and activists had sought to bring these same perspectives to public-school classrooms, after-school programs, and local non-profit organizations. A fledging "youth organizing project," located less than a hundred yards from the largest public high school in Providence, had never generated interest from more than six or seven young people, almost all of whom were young women.

Critical practice seemed to emerge most powerfully from those young men in the Training School. Staff at Broad Street

Studio would sometimes joke about the Training School being a "captive audience" for our workshops. Yet this "captivity" and the pressures it created for young men immersed in the Game of Outlaw seemed to be the conditions necessary for entertaining the possibility of critical practice.

These perspectives challenge young people's habitual orientation to the Game of Outlaw. Rodney discussed the explicitly political lessons imparted by some of his teachers: "And there's also like some teachers that are good in there, but they don't get enough credit for it, you know. Or they'll get told to do the exact opposite. [A teacher will] say, 'Oh I want to teach the last one on the real-life Gettysburg or like, how like, Indians were really tortured,' or something like that—how Rome tried to take over the world. But they'll just tell you, 'Oh the Romans fought a few wars,' but they won't go through the whole subject. These are the people who really need to be out there helping us, you know."

Harmony discussed one teacher's lessons specifically: "I thought Jenny was an excellent teacher, and she might've been the only person I can remember the things I've learned in history. 'His story.' The story that the government wants you to know. But I did remember it. And I didn't remember it to remember it because they wanted me to, I 'membered it to remember how evil and how corrupt shit was...to remember it. She was an excellent teacher."

Anthony remembered, "I did a lot of studying there, lot of social sciences that I really didn't, wasn't too aware of before I got there. But being there made me realize that just because I was arrested for doing something wrong doesn't mean that everyone was locked up actually did something wrong."

Anthony's studies seemed to have helped him develop a political understanding of crime and incarceration.

In addition to what they learned in the Training School classrooms, writing articles for *Hidden TREWTH* also provided young men with a reason to research the issues they cared about in more detail:

MINORITY IMPRISONMENT

> U.S. citizens are 5% of the global population. However, U.S. inmates are 25% of the world's prisoners. Why??? That's the question of the century....It gets worse. Listen to this crazy but true statistic, about 70% of the prisoners in the U.S. are colored people. Did you know that a black male has a 1 in 4 chance of being incarcerated in their life.
> —Ziggy, *Hidden TREWTH*, no. 1 (May 2001)

Ziggy was able to write his article about minority imprisonment based on research that he had requested from us, the newspaper workshop leaders. While Ziggy already had some sense of the injustice of prison policies in the United States, he was able to develop this critique more forcefully through his participation in the newspaper class and was able to use the paper as a platform from which to address other residents.

Laura, Sam, and I were all students at Brown University before working at Broad Street Studio. Over the years, Broad Street Studio has welcomed several other students from local universities. One woman from Providence College ran Broad Street Studio's design program, combining clothing-design workshops with lessons on international sweatshops. Students from the Rhode Island School of Design put together a project in which nearly every resident of the Training School created a tile to represent themselves. And students from an engineering class at Brown put together business plans for several of Broad Street Studio's businesses.

Broad Street Studio was founded by AS220, an organization with a then nearly twenty-year history of providing venues for artistic expression to struggling artists. Expression through the arts was a cornerstone of Broad Street Studio's programming. Several local artists ran workshops for young people at the Training School, and almost all of the staff had some background in an artistic medium. Finally, several staff at Broad Street Studio got involved through their interest in hip-hop and their commitments to working in neighborhoods like the neighborhoods in which they grew up.

MUTUAL RECOGNITION

Young people involved in critical practice find a kind of freedom that is self-reflective, in that they see their own freedom reflected back through the freedom of others. It is useful to compare this with the way that young men make sense of their lives in the Game of Outlaw and the Game of Law. Both the Game of Outlaw and the Game of Law offer young men ways of making sense of themselves through comparisons with other young men. In contrast, those engaging in critical practice make sense of themselves through *identification* with others. For those participating in the Game of Outlaw and the Game of Law, the idea of freedom can be reduced to a strategic freedom—a freedom in terms of the means with which one pursues a conception of masculinity that is not of one's own conscious choosing. For those engaging in critical practice, the goal of young people's activity becomes helping other young people turn away from the Game of Outlaw and toward critical practice itself.

Young people's participation in critical practice is often linked to artistic expression, a medium that allows them to reflect on the society that has constrained them. Rather than entrapping herself by participating in the Game of Outlaw, Harmony suggested, a more effective sort of rebellion came through in her performance: "There's one way they can never incarcerate me ... through poetry and hip-hop, so that's what I do to relieve my stress and relieve my problems about the government. Because I can't just go up to a cop and be like, 'Yo, this is what you do wrong,' but I can ... get on the stage and rhyme about how I feel about it."

Through her artwork, Harmony could vent her rage about social structure at the same time she could influence other young people. Harmony attributed her political understanding to a relationship she established in the Training School with a woman from Broad Street Studio:

> And I mean I've been to jail before, but this time was different. This time was different because, I don't know. I would have to say it just started with the poetry teacher, and that was Erica from Broad Street, which is now my boss [laughs], which now works at where I work. And I don't know, she just started letting me know that my voice was very important. And I always wrote rhymes and wrote poetry and stuff like that, but just letting me know that I had a very powerful voice, and it could be used in more ways than just poetry. It could be used to get messages across that need to be across.... And she started making me realize a lot of things about life. And I didn't like myself anymore as a person. I felt that I was using my voice in the wrong way.

Through her relationship with Erica, Harmony came to see her past behavior as "using her voice in the wrong way," and she began to explore ways in which she could use her skills to address the injustices that she recognized in broader society.

Rodney also seemed to have made a connection between his political understanding and the recognition he has received for his writing:

> Yeah, when I found out I was a real good writer, you know. I felt always that I had a knack for writing, but it just, it never came out that strong until I actually like started studying words, you know. And actually started studying what these words meant, you know, the origins of these words, you know, started reading other people's books, started watching like really, like … movies and stuff that have like, meaning to them, you know, which made me want to say, "Alright, my stuff needs to have meaning behind it too." And when people started coming through from like Broad Street Studio and it was like, "There's money in this, there's money in that." When I just started looking at the places I can be. It's like, "Damn, why be in this situation and waste it when I can be in a situation that's like 100 percent better." And yeah, that's one of them.

Recognized for his writing, Rodney began pushing himself to write things "with meaning." When Broad Street Studio began discussing the possibility of employment for Rodney based on his talent, Rodney became even more interested in rethinking his involvement in the Game of Outlaw.

Similarly, for Anthony, his political consciousness was connected to a recognition of his own talent as a writer, which was rewarded by writing teachers from the outside: "Another major turning point would be meeting you, Dmitri, and Sam, because before that I didn't really take writing too seriously." In all three of the above cases, young people began to recognize the power of their artwork as a way of reflecting on the society that has led so many young people to participate in the Game of Outlaw.

But this new artistic investment does not represent a complete withdrawal from the Game of Outlaw. Rather, the young people who created this artwork saw it as part of a project to help other young people see the "truth" of the Game of Outlaw and the need for participation in critical practice. Rodney and Harmony saw themselves explicitly as leaders with the responsibility to give back to other young people. Rodney expressed the importance of giving back by comparing his own decisions with that of mainstream rap artists:

Rodney: They're not giving back to the hood that they came from. You know.

Adam: Is it important to you to give back?
Rodney: Yeah, it's definitely important. I mean, half of the times I'll have my last dollar left, I'll give it away, you know. Even though, like, damn, I could go out and buy me a drink with this dollar. You know, like get me a nice cold soda. But then I see somebody on the street all with like all busted up clothes, beat up hat. I'm like damn, yo, it's my last dollar if I give it to him. Yeah, I'm gonna be a little dry throat, but then I can always go around the corner to somewhere else and just get a glass of water.

Where rap artists tend to hoard their money, Rodney saw the importance of contributing to the community from which he came. Similarly, Harmony linked the importance of helping others to her own disavowal of criminal activity: "I always think about my past and who I've become now. I think about what I did then and what I do now, and what happens if I become that person again and how I'm gonna destroy what I've done so far because people look up to me."[4]

Rodney and Harmony responded eagerly to a question about what the ideal program would look like for people inside and getting out of the Training School. Rodney answered immediately, "Great, I was hoping you would ask that." He then went on to describe a regimen in which young people were "punished" with education:

> I mean for one, like, soon as they get in, every morning, you know, you kinda like have 'em get up early. And that's one of their punishments—getting up early. You know, to say, you guys are being punished in a certain way. But then we're not gonna punish you by like beatin' your ass, you know, by like bloodying your nose or something like that.... Alright, how 'bout this: five months of education. That's what you're gonna get. You know, I mean, that's the best way I can see how to do it, you know. Instead of saying, "Alright, you're gonna be locked in your room for like three hours a day." I know it sounds silly, but I would do it instead of five days of lockdown, five days of education. Why not?

Both Harmony and Rodney had obviously put some thought into this question before I had asked it. For them, the constituencies with which they identified themselves seemed to have shifted from their peer groups, defined narrowly, to all young people in trouble.

Soon after she began teaching at the facility, Harmony put together a program called Hustler's Prayer, which she described as follows:

> It's a class full of peer education. The peer instructor is a person who's been through things that they've been through, who understands them, who's been in the same position as them before, who teaches them reality and things that are happening in the world for real, not what the media tells you, not what your history books tell you. It uses all those tools to make you look at your own life and what parts you play in the world and how do you want to be in the world. And it helps try to mold people onto the right path. That's what Hustler's Prayer is.

The curriculum Harmony designed was made up of four subjects: politics, history, "the streets," and religion. Within each subject area, Harmony put together several different questions that would be the focus of each lesson: "What is socialism and capitalism, and what are the benefits and problems with each?" "What have other youth in the past done to change history?" "Why do we choose to go through with what we do on the street?" "Where do you think religion came from? Why?" Harmony explained her pedagogy: "I don't want to go into the RITS sounding like a teacher because I'm just like them, I've just turned my life around for the positive with the knowledge I plan to teach them. I've been in their place and I know how hard it can be, wanting to change but not being able to find the right motivation. I want us all to learn together." Hustler's Prayer was, for Harmony, the answer to what was missing in the lives of young people playing the Game of Outlaw.

Young people's commitment to critical practice is, at least in part, a commitment to educating other young people about the insights they have had. This commitment, of course, challenges Training School regulations and staff members' understanding of the Game of Law. There are strict rules limiting former residents' participation at the Training School, given the fear that former residents might bring contraband or outside grudges into the facility. Moreover, most staff seem to equate success with staying as far away from the facility as possible, not voluntarily returning. Harmony was allowed to teach at the Training School six months after release.

Contradictions between the Game of Outlaw and the Game of Law open up the possibility of critical practice for young men in juvenile prison. Young people involved in critical practice maintain their critique of the Game of Law but begin to see their own participation in the Game of Outlaw merely as reproducing their own marginalization. Where young men once aspired toward an unreflective masculinity, with critical practice they instead aspire to a kind of freedom that they can only create with other young people, can only realize in a community of young people who are all reflective about the world they want to inhabit.

The next chapter examines an attempt by young people to establish this kind of world within AS220's Broad Street Studio. As part of the organization, young people worked to realize new forms of family life and work life that broke out of the repressive boundaries of both the Game of Law and the Game of Outlaw.

CHAPTER SIX

Alternative Space and Its Limits

Soon after the new year, in January of 2002, Anthony, Harmony, and a small group of other young people began aggressive distribution of our magazine *Muzine* outside of high schools, at youth organizations, and at events. *Muzine* was Broad Street Studio's outside equivalent to *Hidden TREWTH* and wasn't subject to the administrative regulations of the Training School. Anthony, Harmony, and I had built it from the bottom up, from collecting articles and poems at local schools, to finding advertisers, to conducting interviews. Through AS220 we even found an old anarchist printer who trained us to help out with the printing.

Through small grants and Americorps funding, Anthony, Harmony, and others were able to call this activity "work." Anthony wrote, "Working at AS220 was my first legit job and it opened my eyes to a lot of things. I've lived in Providence my whole life but I never realized how open minded and artist friendly the city is (unless you're a graffiti artist). It was also the first time I realized how hard it is to make a legal dollar.... Getting to see a writer's face when they realize for the first time that their work is actually being published and distributed. Getting feedbacc and constructive criticism on my own writing from my peers."

Anthony and Harmony began running workshops for young people at local public schools as well as at Broad Street Studio. And on one memorable day, in an intentional throwback to the way the Black Panther Party made their early money by selling Mao's *Little Red Book* at Laney College in Oakland, we traveled up College Hill to Brown University to sell the magazine. Only Brown students, Anthony reasoned, would be enamored enough with what we were doing to buy a free magazine for two dollars. Sure enough, we made about forty bucks in less than an hour— not a lot in the grand scheme of things, but enough to make me feel like we had struck gold.

Broad Street Studio is an outgrowth of AS220, a landmark in the Providence arts scene. Umberto Crenca, a white working-class Providence native, founded AS220 in 1985, beginning with eight hundred dollars. The "AS" of AS220 stands for "art space," or "alternative space," and 220 was its initial address, on Wey-bosset Street, a few blocks from two of the large buildings the organization now owns. The organization's budget is now around a million dollars annually.

The cornerstone of AS220's philosophy is the promise of uncensored, unjuried space. Since its opening, any artist has been able to display his or her artwork in its galleries, or perform music on its stage, or use its darkrooms. The waiting list is long, but no one is refused. The organization also offers low-income studio and living spaces for struggling artists and is a hub for all manifestations of the artistic and political fringe. AS220 has been an incubator for several other organizations, from advocacy groups like Youth in Action to Providence's Black Repertory Theater.

I began getting to know Umberto, who goes by "Bert," soon after Laura and I began our work at the Training School. He's a short, stocky man with crows tattooed on both arms and is identified around town as the bald guy with the long, white goatee. His story is one immediately compelling to many of the young men with whom we worked. He had been abusing drugs and was stuck in a life he hated before finding his own vocation as an artist. The eight hundred dollars with which he started AS220 was his lifeline, his last hope for a meaningful life. Like other recovered addicts, he promotes what was his salvation with a kind of missionary zeal. The paradox of Bert's zealotry is that it's in the name of the open, uncensored space in which others can find their own vocations.

Of Italian and Portuguese descent, Bert has politicked his way into the hearts of Providence's ruling class over the course of nearly twenty years. He speaks often of his relationship with Buddy Cianci, the former mayor of Providence, who spent much of the last decade in federal prison on conspiracy charges. During his time in prison, Cianci wrote Bert with the idea that he could perform monologues at AS220 upon his release.

Bert had been offering painting classes at the Training School for at least a year before Laura and I met him. At that point, Broad Street Studio—a transition program for young people released from the Training School—was more fantasy than reality. It was raw potential, a bare warehouse in the South Side, the collection of neighborhoods many residents of the Training

School call home. In the summer of 2001, Bert offered us a small cubicle at the space if we promised to liven it up and work with young people after release. By September, I had taken a job with the studio. The only promise I had to make to Bert was that nothing any young person submitted to our publication would be removed or edited.

In our early conversations, Bert consistently referenced the work of the anarchist Hakim Bey, whose philosophy centered around the possibility of creating temporary autonomous zones, or spaces outside the limits of social structure. Bert's own recent artwork, funny if slightly disturbing creatures Bert refers to as his "friends," demonstrates his own commitment to challenging traditional gender games (see figures 3 and 4).

In the last chapter I outlined the possibility of the emergence of critical practice within the Training School that arose from tensions between the Game of Outlaw and the Game of Law. As part of Broad Street Studio, young people worked to articulate and embody their own conceptions of what work and family should be, outside the dictates of either the Game of Outlaw or the Game of Law. No longer bound to conceptions of masculinity outside of their own reflection, young men (alongside young women) were able to experiment with new, more liberatory forms of social organization.

TRAINING FOR CRITICAL PRACTICE

Just as a person learning to ride a bike must learn through practice—through the mundane, repetitive training of one's body and mind—so must a person learn to change one's orientation to the world. Critical practice did not seem to strike as a bolt of

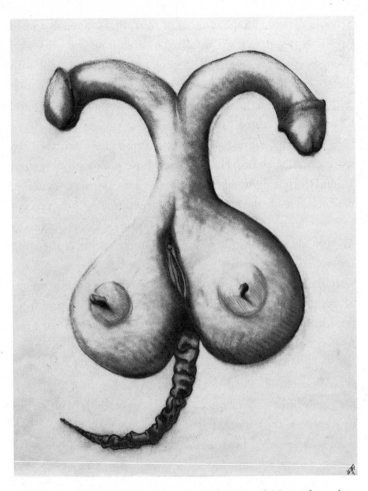

Figure 3. By Umberto Crenca, artistic director of AS220, from the
art show Censored/Uncensored. Photograph by Scott Lapham.

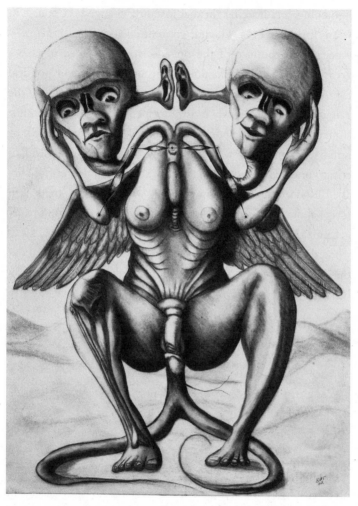

Figure 4. By Umberto Crenca, artistic director of AS220, from the art show Censored/Uncensored. Photograph by Scott Lapham.

lightening, a radical insight that instantly changed the course of young people's lives. Staying committed to critical practice—especially in the face of the outside world—seemed to take a great deal of work. Still, united through artistic and political expression, young men and women found a way to transcend the games that had previously most informed their lives. As demonstrated earlier, this practice did not involve a feeling of guilt or remorse about the past. Indeed, many young people involved in critical practice did not seem to think about their past criminality at all. Rodney discussed how his work with the studio made him forget about the Game of Outlaw entirely: "I mean, I don't really get into trouble anymore. You know, I'm more just like, go to work, do what I have to do. You know, I don't even think about the Training School half of the time. Yeah I do look back on being in there and saying, 'Damn, I can't even believe I was in there.'... Anyway, it's just changed. I don't know man, it's changed a lot. It's hard to explain, you know. Because I got to the point where I don't look at what really changed me, I look at where I'm at now."

Yet critical practice would likely not make it into the outside world at all without organizational form. Scholars have recognized the important role of movement halfway houses during the civil rights movement (Payne 1995), which provided both leadership training as well as emotional resources for those involved. Leaders discussed these organizations as places in which they could practice "being" the way they wanted to be in the world. In a world of racial apartheid, they served as islands within which people could learn to live together.

Broad Street Studio served as this kind of island for many young people. Young people came to identify the space with the new kind of practice in which they were engaged, transcending the boundaries with which young men typically divided up the city. On its best days, Broad Street Studio seemed to carve out its own culture of critical practice, organized around a dedication to creative and political expression. Critical practice was sustained through the creation of an island, an alternative space outside the parameters of the Game of Outlaw or the Game of Law.

SELF-DETERMINATION: REIMAGINING WORK AND FAMILY

As we have seen in previous chapters, both the Game of Outlaw and the Game of Law have specific relationships to work and family. The Game of Outlaw is a rejection of productive work and a separation from the nuclear family. The Game of Law involves a kind of return to an ideal-typical nuclear family in which the man is the head of the household and the breadwinner. Where the Game of Outlaw is a nearly total rejection of both traditional work and the traditional family, the Game of Law is a total acceptance. Neither lets young men or women raise questions about the kinds of work and family lives that would be most fulfilling.

What seemed most notable about Broad Street Studio was the way in which young people deliberately carved out a work and family life that fulfilled them. Harmony recounted when she first heard about the possibility of working at Broad Street Studio, " 'Wow, I can get paid for doing what I love to do. You know what I mean? It's crazy. I have to do this.' You guys all liked my work and you thought it was, you know, good and stuff.

And that's what started making me feel more better about myself and realizing who I was and how important it really was to do things. Broad Street Studio is one of the main things."

She also recalled even more explicitly how the job helped her stay out of the Game of Outlaw once she got out of the Training School. Asked what helped her stay out of trouble, she answered:

> My job, BSS [Broad Street Studio]..., worked there for two years. Started working here what, a week after I got out. Doing *Muzine* with you, Adam. Job is what's kept me there all the way. I mean I wouldn'ta maintained the ideas as a person of what Erica conditioned into me or what I've conditioned myself off of Erica's words. I wouldn'ta been able to maintain it for so long if I didn't have the job showing me things and giving me shows to go do. Things like that. If I didn't have all those things, I wouldn't be where I was. So it's a combined—it's a combination between the fact that Erica's now my boss, and this is the lady that told me words that changed my life around—told me words that I've changed my life around because of based on what she told me and thoughts that I created from what she told me, which is now my boss.

Through spaces like Broad Street Studio, young people were able to put their newfound commitments into practice, which reinforced these commitments outside of juvenile prison. Anthony, similarly, remembered how his work involved the organization and institutionalization of critical practice among other young people: "Actually getting high-school-aged kids to sit in the same room with police officers and feel free to speak their minds on topics such as police brutality and racial profiling was a very big accomplishment. Even though I knew I had nothing to worry about I was still a little hesitant to speak, I guess it's just an ingrained distrust of the police. To tell the truth, being able to work in such a relaxed environment with friends kind of soured me for other jobs."

Staff meetings among young people were not only places to discuss work goals but also opportunities to air personal concerns and receive advice. This was not the forced camaraderie of the "managed heart" (Hochschild 1983), in that young people's emotions were not either "for sale" nor fit within narrow feeling rules. Rather, young people were able to bring to their coworkers, their friends, those parts of their lives that were traditionally separated from the workplace. Charles remembered how important Harmony, and Broad Street Studio more generally, were to his own sense of belonging:

> The Broad Street Studio gave me a sense of belonging a long time ago....So, like [Harmony] she gave me that sense of belonging, that sense of importance. Coming from... She's my own age, I can relate to her, actually she's younger than me, but I can relate to her a lot. As far as I've improved my writing skills, it's helped me as an artist. And it gave me that, since I have confidence as an artist now I have confidence as an individual, because being an artist is a vital part of my life....But it's just like I know that I can always go back, you know, and I can see how everyone's doing, check up with everybody, even though I'm not directly involved with it.

This camaraderie and emotional support extended to the work in which young people engaged together.

The deliberateness with which young people at the studio approached their work together was perhaps in fullest display when the community at the studio established its policy on free speech. During a series of staff meetings, young people debated the tension between their freedom to express their opinions and the need to create a space in which all types of others felt safe. Young people worked together to formulate a "Hater-ation Gets No Toleration" policy, by which they pledged to give each other respect regardless of their backgrounds, genders, races, and sexual orientations. Young men, thus, explicitly rejected the basis on which they gave each other respect in both the Game of Outlaw and the Game of Law.

Throughout my work with Broad Street Studio I was struck by the degree to which young men's stake in proving their masculinity seemed to go into remission. Jerome, a young, black, flamboyantly gay aspiring poet, organized a "Food for Thought" dinner on the topic of homosexuality early in 2002. Several of the young men released from the Training School, many of whom had been making homophobic jokes throughout their stays at the facility, helped recruit other young people for the event and actively participated. Critical practice seemed to demand a less rigid adherence to common conceptions of masculinity, either those of the Game of Outlaw or the Game of Law.

LOSS AND THE LIMITS OF CRITICAL PRACTICE

Loss

I no longer fear death, i wait for the cold
I'm realistic, i don't see myself growing old
Gray hairs and roccin chairs, thatz not for me
All i ask for is a quicc painless death that i don't see
Separated from my better half so itz only half of me

When i die, don't cry just spark up a tree
I've lost so much in such a short ass time
Itz a wonder
I still have the strength to open my eyez
RIP, Jay, MO, Eve and Boy, thatz just this year
How many more gunshots do the young kidz have to hear
When i flow, write, play ball or just drive
I think of fallen soldiers wit tears in my eyez
Life is fucced up!!! why my niggaz have to go
I pray to Allah to take me instead, but i ain't heard bacc
So i guess thatz a no
I've lost love niggaz dream about, movies are written
All i hope for is when i die my sinz are forgiven
Don't judge me on my actionz, or the image i present to
    the world
Base your judgementz on my writingz, and the way i
    viewed the world
When you want to see me again, look at those two
    little girls

—E-mail to author from Anthony,
October 2002

Despite the possibilities of our work together, Jacob's death took a toll on all of us. In its young life, Broad Street Studio had been able to revel in the optimism of new beginnings, without many interventions from the harsher world in which it had carved a space. After Jacob's death, the interventions felt relentless. Less than a month later, another young man with whom many staff members had built relationships was killed only blocks from the studio. Then, in July, the studio was robbed of ten thousand dollars worth of equipment, and it seemed to have been an inside job. The alarm code punched in was the code I had been given, making me and Anthony, with whom I had shared the code, suspect. We were both interrogated at the Providence police station a few blocks from AS220 downtown. Neither one of us ultimately was charged. Nevertheless, Anthony was fired from the studio shortly thereafter. By August, Anthony had fled the state on charges of attempted murder and was staying with relatives in Texas. Rumor was he had been involved in a drive-by shooting in retaliation for Jacob's death. I'd occasionally get a call or e-mail from him, and he expressed fear at what effects it would have on him to go back to jail:

> The thing i miss the most is being in the high schools and workin with other youth. I may be bacc in Prov sooner than expected, i might have to spend some time in jail but fucc it, i honestly don't know how that is gonna affect my demeanor when it comes to life. i don't want to fall bacc in the same negative hole i was in in training school as far as my writing goes. Will i even care about writing when i get out or take it as seriously? i don't even know anymore, itz like at one point in time i was so confident in myself that i would have challenged the sun to a snowball fight, now i can't even go home cuz i don't know how it will affect me to go bacc to jail. Shit is crazy. (E-mail to author from Anthony, October 2002)

He worried about getting caught back in a "negative hole," about not caring about writing anymore. In the poem he sent me along with the e-mail, "Loss," he asks not to be judged by his actions but by his writings and suggests that his two daughters are the legacy he'd be leaving. Ultimately he did return to Rhode Island, and he was arrested and convicted soon after. Anthony wrote from prison,

> The most rewarding moment I've ever had at AS220 was helping my man Jacob get a job at BSS. It felt good to be able to follow through instead of just talking about it. I'd

known Jacob since his family moved to Providence from the
Bronx and we'd always run into either other, either on the
streets with both of us doing our own thing or in the
Training School. Unfortunately, little over a month after he
started, Jacob was shot to death a few bloccs down from
Broad St. Studio. The investigation into his murder is still
open, as much good as that will do, every action has an
equal and opposite reaction. Though I continued to work
for AS220 for 8 months after Jacob's death, I never really
put the same energy into it. No matter how much you may
want to leave the street life alone, there may be someone
you have wronged in the past who may see things differently. You can't control the actions of others. (Letter to
author from Anthony, July 2005)

THE FRAGILITY AND POSSIBILITY
OF CRITICAL PRACTICE

The structural possibility of critical practice did not exist on the
outside—rather, it had to be constructed through organization.
Broad Street Studio was, and is, a small organization compared
with the strength of both the Game of Outlaw and the Game of
Law. Staff constantly struggled with simply getting young people
to show up to work on time.

Even at an organization like AS220's Broad Street Studio,
critical practice is difficult to sustain. Like other not-for-profit
organizations, it relies almost entirely on funding from foundations. This has different sorts of inhibiting effects on the possibilities for critical practice. First, the reliance on outside
funding means that foundations inevitably have some control
over the agenda of Broad Street Studio. It also means that young

people ultimately have relatively little power in the organization's agenda setting, in spite of the communal staff meetings and the staff's real commitment to young people "having a voice" (see Pfeffer and Salancik 1978). This was made clear when Broad Street Studio won a large grant from an antitobacco campaign funded by tobacco settlement money. Much of the studio's artwork, from its clothing design to its performances, related to the antitobacco campaign, an issue of only marginal significance to many of the young people involved. Many would take cigarette breaks from their work on these art projects.

Still, according to Sam Seidel, the director of Broad Street Studio during the antitobacco campaign, the studio worked to balance its own agenda with the realities of existing streams of funding, trying to "pimp the system" to make critical practice possible despite funding constraints. About the tobacco money, Sam remembered that "we didn't go for the whole grant" but only applied for "the part that involves using art and lifting young people's voices to criticize and shed light on the ways corporations and society exploit and prey on poor young people of color in urban environments." Sam went on to list ways in which the studio made use of foundation and state money to do "transgressive, transformative stuff," arguing that there were "large areas where we weren't explicitly violating rules but we were still ... helping young people see flaws in the system." Just as young people involved in critical practice learned to perform differently for different audiences, Sam suggested that the staff of the studio was able to "code switch" with funders and state agencies to provide resources for critical practice. Nevertheless, it seems like there are natural limits to this sort of under-the-radar practice. To the extent that young people are truly and visibly coming to challenge existing configurations of power, these sources of funding seem likely to dry up.

Second, the studio's reliance on foundation support puts it in implicit, and sometimes explicit, competition with many of the other small not-for-profit organizations working with young people in Providence, many of which apply for the same grants. Where the boundaries between gang territories became less relevant at Broad Street Studio, the boundaries between not-for-profit groups became salient. Sam again downplayed this limitation, arguing that he and other similar nonprofit organizations came to realize that they were "doing different things" and so could maintain a cordial and sometimes collaborative relationship with one another. Yet this same imperative for nonprofit groups to distinguish themselves from one another—serving slightly different constituencies in slightly different ways—seems to stand in the way of a larger political voice for young people as a whole.

Finally, organizations with 501c(3) status are explicitly barred from engaging in lobbying or any electoral political activity. While young people from Broad Street Studio would often participate in conferences or discussions with public officials, they were not permitted to engage in any overt challenges to political authority. The critical practice in which young people did participate was mostly one of political expression and not the building of political power.

These observations raise the question of how marginalized young people might be able effectively to build political power within a city or within the country as a whole. A cynical perspective is offered by scholars who suggest that gang violence is *itself* a mechanism through which neighborhoods leverage resources from city governments (Jankowski 1991) or who suggest that the only resource with which the lower class can leverage power is rioting: "Many among the lower class are in locations that make their cooperation less than crucial to the operation of major institutions. Those who work in economically marginal enterprises, or who perform marginally necessary functions in major enterprises, or those who are unemployed, do not perform roles on which major institutions depend. Indeed, some of the poor are sometimes so isolated from significant institutional participation that the only 'contribution' they can withhold is that of quiescence in civil life: they can riot" (Piven and Cloward 1977: 25).

In order to prove these scholars wrong, new strategies need to be formulated for effective leveraging of power among young people. To a certain extent, it seems that political understanding may *itself* transform the political opportunities available to a constituency, as when the citizens of Montgomery began identifying the bus fare as a resource with which to leverage power against bus companies, or when civil rights organizers recognized the advantages of subjecting themselves to white violence (McAdam 1982). But in the poorest neighborhoods in our cities, there is currently little support even for the processes that would help young people identify the modern-day equivalent of the bus fare.

Conclusion

Critical Practice and Public Policy

I would like to be able to conclude with a clear public-policy agenda, a concise statement outlining what can be done to break the cycle of young men's crime and incarceration. This same desire to tie up loose ends is perhaps what motivated me to spend the last several months of my time in Rhode Island working as a consultant for the state's Department of Children, Youth, and Families. The Training School had been in legal trouble with the state for over twenty years, but juvenile justice reform was finally on the state's agenda. With my colleague at Broad Street Studio, Sam Seidel, we worked to compile best thinking on the directions the state should move.

We were not sensitive to the fact that "best thinking" almost never drives juvenile correctional policy. This time around, the impetus for reducing the number of young people incarcerated in Rhode Island was Cranston mayor Stephen P. Laffey, who "ha[d] long wanted to move the Training School farther away from the Garden City neighborhood," a growing shopping complex (*Providence Journal*, April 29, 2003). A sewer line regularly overflowed into the proposed site for the Training School, a small lot about a mile down the road. And for any new structure to be built there, more than a thousand bodies in a historical "pauper's cemetery" would have to be moved (*Providence Journal*, October 2, 2003). A unit manager at the Training School did not seem far off when he observed, "Nobody cares about these kids around here, all they care about here is building more and more developments. Last thing they want to see is the Training School with the big ugly fence around it. They want to stick us down the street in a mud hole somewhere so they can take this land and put another strip mall in it."

Sam and I jumped at the possibility of contributing to a reform effort that would reduce the number of young men and women in custody, regardless of why the political opportunity arose. But those invested in shutting down the current facility were not necessarily allies in imagining a more just system. Our presentation to stakeholders in early January of 2005 fell mostly on deaf ears. And despite the best efforts of several progressive juvenile-program workers and community allies, the opening of the new facility seemed to represent a shift in geography more than a shift in philosophy for juvenile corrections in the state.

I had found a more receptive audience in maximum security a few months before. I was running on empty, having just filed my undergraduate thesis, and explained to the class of six guys why I was a little more haggard than usual. They immediately wanted to know the contents of what I had written. We tossed the lesson plan to the wind and for the next hour re-created the thesis together. I asked them why they got involved in crime, how the Training School affected their thinking, and what they thought the future held for them. And as they shouted out answers, I began to spell out elements of the argument I have made in this book. As I neared the conclusion, the atmosphere changed from the give-and-take of an academic discussion to something more closely resembling a sermon. I argued that young men's best hope for rehabilitation was to commit themselves to the redemption of the social world that led them to crime in the first place. Heads nodded in silence, and for the first time in three years of classes with these young men—discussing writing, poetry, politics, and everything in between—I felt as if I had taught them something almost as valuable as what they had taught me.

THE CONTRADICTIONS OF CRIMINOLOGY

How, then, to think about the contribution academic work such as this can make to substantive changes in young men's lives? Below, I outline how the lessons of *Hidden Truth* complicate existing theories of delinquency. I also suggest that this book has implications for thinking differently about the mechanism by which juvenile correctional reform might take place and about the actors who will bring it about. I continue to believe that young men's individual rehabilitation must be connected to the collective rehabilitation of the world in which they live. To avoid the dual reproductions of outsider masculinity and insider masculinity, the challenge is for organizers, teachers, and young men themselves to create the space for critical practice.

Beyond Deterrence and Disease

Debate over juvenile correctional policy tends to focus on the question of punishment and deterrence versus treatment and rehabilitation. Classical criminologists (Beccaria 1764/1819; Bentham 1811/1830), like modern-day conservatives (see Wilson 1983), consider all individuals as autonomous, economically rational decision makers. Crime is a natural human tendency, since—absent sanction—its benefits outweigh its costs. By increasing the costs of criminal behavior, legal sanctions are able to reduce the amount of crime in a society.

The positivist turn in criminology was an understandable but ultimately unsatisfying response to the deficiencies of the classical perspective—in many ways consistent with standard progressive accounts of crime. The positivist tradition encompasses a wide range of theories united by the idea that crime is not rational but rather a pathological and indirect product of either biological or environmental factors. Whether criminals inherit "defects" (e.g., Lombroso 1911), or are made pathological through environmental factors (e.g., Quetelet 1833), the positivist school posits that criminals have very little control over their own actions. What the positivist tradition captures well is the seemingly irrational behavior exhibited by some criminals. Moreover, its evolution from biological to environmental factors shows the beginnings of an awareness of the social structures within which criminality takes place.

If we return to Luis, the soft-spoken young man who explained how he "had to be crazy," that there was "only one way," we can begin to understand the inadequacies of both of classical and positivist criminology. The young men who enact outsider masculinity do make choices in ways they understand as reasonable and rational, but theirs is reason that bears little relationship to the economic costs and benefits discussed by classical criminologists. Rather, strategic displays of "craziness" are part of how young men can prove their masculinity in a world that denies them institutional power. The deterrents that classical criminologists suggest, then, may factor into young men's decisions in "logical" ways but may only reinforce the premium given displays of craziness. Even incarceration may be framed as a badge of honor within the Game of Outlaw.

On the other hand, offering these young men psychological treatment, as if their behavior were a result of pathology, fails to engage with the quite coherent world of rules and meanings within which these young men live. Where the classical perspective abstracts rationality outside of a specific set of ends and meanings, the positivist perspective abandons it altogether.

Beyond the Peer Group

Another policy solution has been simply to remove young offenders from the neighborhoods from which they came and to embed them with other noncriminal young people. This solution roots the problem of criminality in the peer group and suggests that a young man has a better chance to leave criminality behind when he leaves his compatriots behind as well.

This policy argument derives from a subcultural perspective on delinquency. This view breaks from the classical and positivist traditions with its focus on the peer group (Matza 1964; Merton 1968; Cloward and Ohlin 1960). Yet this perspective, in many ways an extension of the positivist school, falls into many of its same pitfalls, emphasizing an abstract "culture of criminality." This is an advance from classical and positivist criminality in that it understands criminality as being connected to the meanings that young men create together. Yet it largely fails to interrogate the connections between this peer group and the social world from which it springs. Subculturalists risk treating crime as if it were an exotic tribal practice into which young men are seduced. And in attributing agency to the group over the individual, this perspective tends to lose track of how the group itself emerged and also minimizes the role of individual young men in its emergence. These theorists focus on the ideological characteristics of the criminal group at the expense of an analysis of the specific political and economic positions from which criminals confront the social world.

Kevin's story reveals the paradoxes in this perspective. A black sixteen-year-old, Kevin had just been released from the Training School when we met up for an interview. I ask him how he had become involved in crime:

Kevin: Hanging with the wrong people. Then doing everything they wanted to do. Not following though, leading into what they wanted to do. But not following.

Adam: What do you mean?
Kevin: 'Cause I don't follow nobody. They all follow me.

Kevin initially acknowledged the influence of his peers yet immediately contradicted himself, asserting that he actually was the leader, "leading into what they wanted to do." When asked to provide a motivation for his own participation in crime, he asserted simultaneously that he was a follower and a leader. The subcultural literature is similarly unsatisfying. If everyone follows, and even the leaders "lead into what [others] wanted to do," where does the criminal peer group come from in the first place?

Moreover, the subcultural viewpoint explains criminality by dismissing the commonsense understandings of criminals themselves. Young criminals' espousal of a "criminal identity," for example, is reduced to evidence of labeling (Mead 1934; Becker 1963), a process through which the legal stigma of criminality reinforces criminal identities by reifying the boundary between the law and its "outsiders."

The concept of outsider masculinity helps us see that young men construct a masculinity game among their peers but that this game is intimately connected with masculinity games played by men with greater social power. Young men prove their masculinity as individuals, as "leaders," but this outsider notion of masculinity requires a group to give it recognition. Crime depends on young men believing that they must prove their masculinity individually at the same time that it requires a group within which to assert this individualism. Young men's espousals of radical individualism, then, are themselves a product of a kind of agreement to abide by the rules of the game.

Beyond Pure Critique

A final trend in the literature, perhaps especially common among sociologists and others slightly more removed from the everyday concerns of policy makers, is to argue that nothing short of social revolution will prevent certain socially marginal young men from engaging in crime.

This point of view reacts against the myopia of the subculturalist perspective and draws attention instead to the macro structures that determine the very definitions of crime. Alvin Gouldner (1973: 37), for example, argues that the study of the subculture of deviance "expresses the satisfaction of the Great White Hunter who has bravely risked the perils of the urban jungle to bring back an exotic specimen." Those more radical criminologists with whom Gouldner might be sympathetic propose that we understand the definition and punishment of crime as resulting from forces of production and a bourgeoisie concerned with preserving social stability or maintaining a stable workforce (Rusche and Kirscheimer 1939; Young 1999).

Criminals, in this model, are the products of forces entirely beyond their control. The way these criminals see the social world is irrelevant to the perpetuation of this world. The consciousness and activity of criminals are caused by social structures rather than being included as *part of* the structures made the object of analysis. This tendency in the literature is only made more explicit by the small group of radical scholars (e.g., Fanon 1963) who take seriously the consciousness of the criminal. These scholars argue that the criminal's marginal position in relationship to the economy makes revolutionary consciousness and activity inevitable. They see an almost mechanical relationship between the criminal's position in the forces of production and his political understanding and practice. Again, for these scholars, the consciousness and practices of the criminal are the *result* of their position in the social structure rather than understood as a part of that social structure. For critical criminologists, the criminal group—whether pawns or a revolutionary lumpen proletariat—is just one more product of economic forces.

This perspective has a great deal of resonance with what I call *pure critique* in the preceding analysis. As I have argued, young men involved in crime tend to have a sophisticated critique of the broader social world yet one that fails to see their own criminal involvement as a reproduction of this social world. One of the earliest poems Anthony published in *Hidden TREWTH* was a moving tribute to the possibility of political change:

> Everyone is too busy tryin to be the first on
> Their blocc wit the new car
> If I was to look in the sky
> So I could wish on one star
> I'd wish for everyone to try and change the way thingz are
> —Anthony, *Hidden TREWTH*, no. 1 (May 2001)

Reading over the poem before publication, however, I noticed that Anthony had replaced every "ck" with a "cc" and had crossed out the blank space in every "b." I learned that since he identified with the Folk Nation gang, an East Coast affiliate of the Crips, he refused to use "ck," which in gang slang is an abbreviation for "Crip Killer." The "b" stood for the Blood gang, the Folks' enemies. The contradiction embedded in Anthony's poem seemed a failure on Anthony's part to treat his own consciousness—his own way of seeing the world—as a *part* of the social structures he criticized. He wished for everyone "to try and change the way thingz are" but was not willing to abandon his own allegiance to a gang that perpetuated the world as he knew it.

Outsider masculinity seems to prevent a reflection on the conditions of its emergence. In other words, playing the Game of Outlaw makes it difficult to see the contours of the social structure from which the game has emerged. Crime seems to some extent to require a mindless allegiance to its rules and blindness to the social structure within which it exists. To the extent that young men are reflective about the ends or ultimate purposes of criminal involvement, they seem *less* likely to participate in crime at all.

CRITICAL PRACTICE AND
THE HIDDEN TRUTH

For some young men, the collision of the Game of Outlaw and the Game of Law at the Training School leads to a kind of transcendence of both, in which achieving masculinity loses some of its motivational power. For these young men, the acquisition of "money, power, and respect" becomes less important than the collective transformation of their own neighborhoods and lives. Money becomes merely a way to meet one's basic needs. Power becomes something not to exert individually over others but rather to use collectively to create a more just world. And respect becomes something mutually given and received rather than "won." The young men who engage in critical practice leave crime behind but do not merely turn to insider masculinity that reproduces their own economic marginality. Rather, they emerge from the Training School committed, with others, to challenge the broader social structures that constitute insider and outsider masculinity in the first place. Their individual change is connected to the change they work to enact in the world.

The challenge facing these young men, and the people who care about and work with them, is how to foster critical practice, how to encourage young men's critiques of the social world while challenging their investment in an outsider masculinity that merely reproduces their marginality. How do we connect young men's critiques with practices and organizations that sustain critical practice while in a world that rewards outsider *and* insider masculinity so much more easily? And how do we sustain hope for critical practice when social change is so hard to come by and when examples of failure are so much more numerous than those of success?

Meeting this challenge seems to entail, at least in part, a search for those cracks and fissures in which to create the space for critical practice. Sam remarks that he "doesn't feel like many people are doing" the work of Broad Street Studio but that they could be, since states at least nominally still have rehabilitative obligations to young people, and yet state bureaucracies tend not to keep too close an eye on how these obligations are met. Nationally, as the costs of incarceration have come to overwhelm state budgets, there seems to be at least some political space for diverting money from incarceration to programs that might prevent incarceration. In this regard, bipartisan organizations like the Council of State Governments have done impressive work in some of the most conservative states of the country.[1]

For me, maintaining hope in the face of evidence to the contrary is the most difficult challenge to wrap my head around. Hope is something somewhat counterintuitive in social science, which tends to spend much more time focusing on explaining what *did* happen than what *might have* happened. Something unlikely, regarded statistically as one time in twenty, is dismissed outright. Yet moments of critical practice are more likely to give way to social reproduction than they are to transform the social world. Outsider masculinity and insider masculinity do not easily give way in these young men's lives.

EPILOGUE AS PROLOGUE

In March of 2005, Anthony wrote from adult prison with news of his newborn son, his namesake: "I don't know if I told you already but my son was born in November…I'm done now, thatz it 4 me, I got my prince I'm good. When I get home I got four little mez to answer to…I just can't afford to slip anymore, therez 4 lives out there that I'm directly responsible for."

He discussed the weight of his responsibility for four lives, how he "can't afford to slip anymore." He expressed a desire to be a good breadwinner. Anthony seemed to have convinced himself to eschew outsider masculinity once and for all, yet the possibility of critical practice no longer enticed him. Rather, he seemed ready to adopt the insider masculinity he had previously shunned. In another letter, he explicitly disowned the political critique that had been so important to him: "I think I'm about done with rebellion, once my children are financially secure then I'll think about trying to overthrow the government until then I'm trying to stay under the radar. Fucc prison, these mothafuccaz will never see me again" (letter to author from Anthony, April 2005).

By "rebellion," Anthony again seemed to conflate breaking the law with "overthrow[ing] the government." He still recognized the futility of outsider masculinity but also seemed to have abandoned critical practice, inching instead toward the Game of Law:

> People can say what they want, who cares if I'm the craziest
> nigga from the South Side, if I'm in jail for life and can't
> feed my kidz what good is street credibility. My children
> can't eat from that, I can't walk into a store and say I'm
> Wyzdom from the South Side, I'm broke but you're gonna
> give me that case of baby formula and some diapers cuz I'm
> Wyz. I'm good, I'm a leave that shit to the young niggaz
> who don't have kidz or to the ones that haven't opened
> their eyes yet. (Letter to author from Anthony,
> March 2005)

Anthony recognized he could not buy baby formula with street credibility. His goals had narrowed from the transformation of the society in which he lives to basic provision for his children. He decided he "can't do to [his] kids what [his] father did to [him]." And yet he still seemed to take some pride in his legacy as the "craziest nigga from the South Side," still planned to "grow weed in [his] backyard."

Over the course of his time in prison, Anthony's letters to me also revealed a deepening religious faith. The first line of his letter to me in April of 2005 was, "Adam, Whatz hood, howz everything with you?" This was in marked contrast to his greeting of February 2006: "As Salaamu Alaikum Wa Rahmatullahi Wa Barakatuh (Peace be upon you and the Mercy of Allah and His Blessings) [sic]." In prison Anthony had become a Sunni Muslim and prayed five times a day.

In June of 2009, I returned to Providence to meet with Anthony and Harmony about the upcoming publication of this book. Anthony had been released from adult prison a little over a year before, was living with his girlfriend and the mother of two of his children, and had found a few temporary positions—

most recently he'd been packing frozen squid. I met him where he was living, about three blocks from the spot we met when he was first released from the Training School. He said he'd been more of a homebody recently, doing dishes and taking care of the kids at least some of the time.

Given his newfound religious faith, and the time that had elapsed since we'd last spoken, I was surprised by how familiar it felt to be together. As we drove to court to pay restitution fines on the second-degree robbery for which he had been convicted, Anthony critiqued the justice system that had imprisoned him for several years only to leave him thousands of dollars in debt. He berated the parole board in Rhode Island, which he argued was illegal since several of its members had served well beyond state term limits. He was the same Wyzdom, only now twenty-five. And now, as he put it, he was willing to be "a civilian," which was "much harder than being a criminal" since he now had to work fifty hours a week for four hundred dollars.

Anthony and Harmony had been in touch with one another sporadically since his release. So while I hadn't been able to get in touch with Harmony by phone before my visit to the city, Anthony knew where she was living and thought it would be okay to stop by. We woke her up with a knock at her apartment in Pawtucket, and after initially refusing us she begrudgingly dressed and joined us for breakfast at a local diner. Pretty soon, as Harmony said, "it felt just like 2002."

For the past few years Harmony had been working in customer service for a major insurance company, dealing with customers' disability claims. Before that she worked briefly servicing mortgages. She now had a three-year-old daughter and a live-in boyfriend who took care of her daughter while she was at work.

She explained that he stayed home because he could never make as much money as she did. Still, she didn't get health insurance through her job, the premium for which would have taken too much of a bite into her monthly paycheck.

Anthony said that he had eschewed any ties with people who might get him into trouble. Harmony still mentored younger members of the Blood gang but said she mostly focused on helping them with job applications and ways to support themselves without resorting to crime. Both Anthony and Harmony have continued to write music and spent part of our afternoon together sharing their latest work with me and with one another. It's still impressive, still smart and catchy, but it had a different feel than it did when we used to work together. Writing about politics was just "too sad" now, Harmony said. She focused instead on writing what "people wanted to hear," on getting people dancing. Anthony's writing had also lost its political edge. And for the first time in his life, he said he had writer's block.

The last song Anthony played for me before we left Harmony's apartment was called "Did You Hold It Down?" It was slower and softer than his other songs and described how he had been let down by his friends and family while he was in prison. He said it had led to a three-hour argument with his mom and that he had ultimately taken it down from his personal Web site because he had "gotten in too much trouble" for it. While Anthony had been remarkably consistent in our friendship while he was in adult prison, my letters had become less and less frequent. Without saying as much, he seemed to be letting me know that I had let him down.

What has happened to the other young people with whom I worked? A few have managed to stay out of prison. But like

Harmony and Anthony since his most recent release, they have done so by reinserting themselves within the Game of Law. Charles has stayed out of prison since his release in 2003. When we last spoke he was attending a college readiness program and learning computer-programming skills. Martin was still working to support his wife and two young children. For all of these young people, Broad Street Studio was a launching pad from crime back to the Game of Law. Given the high rates of return at the Rhode Island Training School and Adult Correctional Institution, staying out of prison is perhaps success enough. But as is clear in these young people's stories, critical practice takes a back seat to more pressing everyday concerns. Harmony, Charles, and Martin—the only young people I know to have avoided adult prison entirely—are all white.

Several other young men with whom I worked have returned to the Game of Outlaw and have spent time in adult prison. Rodney, Joshua, Richard, and others have all spent time at the Adult Correctional Institution down the road from the Training School. Richard wrote to me from prison. His understanding of his life seemed strikingly similar to young men in the Training School who asserted that they have learned the errors of their ways and have committed to the Game of Law:

> Up until this point in my life I would tell people that I've made a lot of mistakes that can't be taken bacc, however I can and did learn from them. In order to make it to the top you have to fall down, at least that's what I think. The most important turning point in my life was when I realized that if I don't change my behavior then I'll be in and out of prison my whole life. Knowing this if I choose to go out and do the same things again I'd be stupid. Another thing

that woke me up was when I was at a visit with my pregnant
wife. I realized that it's not only me I'm hurting anymore, I
hurt them by being here too. (Letter to author from
Richard, August 2006)

I had seen a similar kind of regret among those young people
in juvenile prison who were quick to distance themselves from
the Game of Outlaw. Yet, like so many other young people,
Richard likely underestimated his attraction to the Game of
Outlaw upon release. Indeed, he admitted that his involvement
in crime had made him who he was, which raised questions for
me about the degree to which he was willing to leave it behind:
"I'm not gonna blame my incarceration on my parents or anyone
else. I'm the one who made the choices I did so I'm the one to
blame. I'm the one who decided to join a street gang so I have
to accept the consequences of it. If I would have chose to go
down a different path I would have probably never gotten into
trouble. I don't regret anything I did because everything I did is
what makes me, me" (letter to author from Richard, August
2006). Richard proclaimed his intention to live out the Game of
Law on the outside, not to keep in contact with anyone other
than his wife and sister. He committed to following a life of
marriage and work, in keeping with the insider masculinity pro-
moted by the Training School. Like some of the young men in
chapter 2, he took responsibility entirely for his own decisions.

Like Anthony, others seemed to find a deeper religious faith
in prison, which itself seemed to be a version of insider masculinity. Joshua illustrated this religious faith most clearly:

Adam, May Peace Be Unto You. I hope this response finds
you in the best of health and with a humble heart. Insha

Allah. At the time I was insecure and unsure of my goals, strengths, identity (natural, at such a point in one's life. Identities are usually challenged and created often, right?!), and I also lacked great amount of discipline....I am a Muslim as Harif (Anthony) may have related to you. So, we may speak from a Muslim point of view of course. We are men and we have flaws and strengths, desires and discipline. (Letter to author from Joshua, August 2006)

Joshua's religious practice seemed another way to reassert his masculinity, a way of feeling in control of his life in prison at the same time he asserted himself as a "man" with "flaws and strengths."

None of the men currently incarcerated in adult prison with whom I have corresponded expressed the desire to continue participating in the Game of Outlaw. In Paul Willis's study (1977), the young men who have rebelled against school and glorified the manliness of the factories find themselves trapped working in the factories as adults. It was only after they reproduced their own subjugation that they were able to see it clearly. Likewise, the adults in prison expressed disappointment with their own youthful stupidity, yet many now have long prison sentences.

Despite these persistent reproductions, if this study suggests anything it is that those identities to which young men subscribe most strongly—identities wrapped up in the games that make them men—are contingent and changeable, and that there exists latent possibility for their transformation even in those environments in which they seem to reign supreme. While he was incarcerated, Anthony had pushed me to turn our work together into this book and had sent me a detailed plan for the marketing and promotion of the finished work. Among other things, he suggested that it be an "ongoing, interactive project." And while this medium does not lend itself to that format, in many ways I wish it did. All of the young people in this work are still relatively young. To predict their ongoing confinement in prison, or in the world of low-wage work, feels premature.

One might argue that Anthony and my stories—and the contents of this book more generally—are only evidence of the persistence with which the social world reproduces itself. I, the son of two academics, have used my work with young offenders as fodder for my own academic trajectory. Anthony, born into poverty and violence, reproduced this violence and wound up in adult prison. This reading, however, seems to discount the real possibility for critical practice emerging inside the Training School and out. That this possibility may realize itself imperfectly, or in fits and starts, is not reason to dismiss it entirely. By describing what I see as the tensions inherent in the games that young men play in order to prove themselves men, and the possibility that these games may be transcended, I hope to make more possible this transcendence and the emergence of critical practice.

NOTES

INTRODUCTION

1. In this book I have tried to balance the ethical responsibility of the scholar to preserve the anonymity of his or her subjects, on the one hand, with a desire to honor and recognize those whom I respect and admire, on the other. One of the paradoxes of academic work dealing with marginalized people is that it risks reproducing their anonymity in the name of subjects' "protection." With their permission, then, I have left unchanged the names of Anthony and Harmony, two of the young people (now in their midtwenties) whose stories make up the core narrative of the book. I have also left unchanged the name of Jacob Delgado, in whose memory the book is dedicated, as well as the names of my colleagues at Broad Street Studio: Laura Rubin, Sam Seidel, and Umberto Crenca. When I excerpt writing published in *Hidden TREWTH*, I have used the name or tag published, unless this writing is by someone who appears at other places in the text. In every other instance, however, I have changed the names of the young people with whom I worked and the names of those interviewed in order to preserve their anonymity.

2. In the spirit of young people's unfiltered expression, we often left grammatical and spelling errors uncorrected while editing *Hidden TREWTH*. Throughout this book, where I have cited poetry and articles from the newspaper, I have maintained this practice.

3. Rhode Island Department of Children, Youth and Families, Rhode Island Child Information System (RICHIST) data for 2008. There were also small percentages of residents who identified as Asian (3%), Native American (1%), multiracial (2%), and quite a number who were of "unknown race" (16%).

4. On review of this manuscript, Anthony suggested that while juvenile records are formally sealed, and so cannot be viewed by the public, prosecutors and other state officials still often invoke these records in arguing for stricter sentencing after young people reach the age of majority.

5. Data courtesy of the Rhode Island Training School.

6. Data from a 2001 report compiled by the Providence Plan, *Census 2000: The Changing Face of Providence*, www.providenceplan.org/cen2000 (site discontinued).

7. According to RICHIST data, while twenty young men were incarcerated at the Training School for felony assault in January of 2008, none were incarcerated for murder.

8. This is consistent with theorists who argue that masculinity can be understood as a need to distinguish oneself from others (Freud 1930/1961; Chodorow 1978); as strict adherence to and high regard for impersonal rules (Lever 1976); as a competitive and strategic orientation to other people (Thorne 1993); and as a tendency to organize people into hierarchies (Connell 1987).

9. When interview dialogue appears in the text, I distinguish between interviews I conducted (where my name appears as the one speaking) and interviews conducted by research assistants (where an "Interviewer" is speaking).

10. Connell begins to do this herself with her distinction between hegemony, complicity, and subordination on the one hand, and authority and marginalization on the other (Connell 1995: 80). Yet this second

axis of power (authority/marginalization) never feels fully incorporated into her theory.

11. One serious risk in the contemporary masculinities literature is that masculinities get defined as those ways that men behave. In this case, the concept of "masculinity" becomes both tautological (Hood-Williams 2001) and inextricably linked to men's bodies, meaning that there is no way for distinguishing masculinity from the variety of things that men do, and no room for women to be understood as masculine (see Pascoe 2007). If we are serious about the concept of masculinity (as distinct from the concept of "men"), we need to give the concept some meaning beyond being those things that men do.

12. Like recent scholarship on gender, this approach highlights the importance of practice in the making and ongoing remaking of masculinity (West and Zimmerman 1991; Butler 1993).

13. One of the most valuable insights of later Freud and the Frankfurt School is that the instrumental rationality that exemplifies the meaning of masculinity can, at its limit, substitute means for ends: one's energy can become so focused on competing that one stops questioning why one competes at all. The most interesting gender scholarship to have explored this point is Jessica Benjamin's *The Bonds of Love* (1988). Benjamin (186ff.) observes how the arenas of emotional connection and intersubjective recognition are relegated to the "feminine" private sphere, which itself becomes the object of a separate, calculating, public masculinity. A public, masculine ethic of "means" then comes to dominate a private, feminine ethic of "ends." Reasoning becomes disconnected from values—with the former coded masculine and the latter coded feminine.

14. Within Bourdieu's world of ubiquitous game playing, the only way that social change may occur is if people who were part of one game become part of another in which they do not have the same investment. How is this possible, given his theory that the games people play derive from their position in social space? For Bourdieu, people's investments are formed early in life, which means that it is possible to have a "hysteresis effect" in which people come (through changes in the

world of which they are a part) to apply practices learned in the past to a changed environment (for the best account of "hysteresis," see Bourdieu 1990: 54ff.). Bourdieu offers little account of when his "hysteresis effect" is more or less likely to occur and implies that there is nothing more or less "accurate" about the way people relate to the social world with or without this effect.

15. Judith Lorber (2005: xx) argues that we should work toward a world "without gender all the time," in which people feel free to challenge and play with existing gender categories and meanings (see also Butler 1993).

PART I

1. Rhode Island Department of Children, Youth and Families, Rhode Island Child Information System (RICHIST) data for 2007.

2. RICHIST data for January 14, 2008.

CHAPTER 1

1. See Howard Becker's *Outsiders* (1963) for a discussion of labeling theory.

2. Rhode Island is one of a very few states in which this is true. In 2008, a bill passed the state assembly that would have released someone convicted of violation of probation but was then exonerated or acquitted of the charge leading to the probation violation. This bill was vetoed by the governor (*Providence Journal*, March 21, 2009).

CHAPTER 2

1. This is consistent with psychoanalytic theories of masculinity that suggest that young men understand themselves as men by seeking autonomy and separation from a female caregiver (Chodorow 1978).

2. For more on Harmony and her relationship to masculinity, see the introduction to part 3.

3. See Randall L. Kennedy's discussion (1999/2000) of the history of the word *nigger*, and its different meanings in different contexts.

PART II

1. For an interesting discussion of how the lack of structure can perpetuate existing race and gender inequalities, see Jo Freeman's "The Tyranny of Structurelessness" (1972–73).

CHAPTER 3

1. Rhode Island Department of Children, Youth and Families, Rhode Island Child Information System (RICHIST) data for 2008. Of Training School residents, 49 percent were reportedly between the ages of sixteen and seventeen, while 28 percent were between the ages of eighteen and twenty. These older residents had likely either been arrested under the age of eighteen, and were serving out their sentences, or had violated parole and were being returned to the Training School instead of the Adult Correctional Institution.

2. RICHIST data for 2003.

3. The California Youth Authority, for example, is one of the most notoriously violent and disorganized juvenile corrections systems in the country.

4. The Texas Youth Authority, for example, implemented a resocialization program in the mid-1990s that closely regulated the actions and interactions of residents in custody.

5. The Training School is what James Q. Wilson (1989) calls a "coping organization," in which supervisors can observe neither the outputs nor outcomes of its key operators. In this type of environment it is almost impossible for administrators to hold accountable teachers, juvenile-program workers, social workers, and everyone else that come

into direct contact with young people, for either what they do or what effect their actions have.

CHAPTER 4

1. That being said, one important difference between fights inside and out is the absence of guns inside the Training School. Several years after Jacob's death, one staff member at Broad Street Studio suggested to me that he thought Jacob—only recently released from the Training School at the time he was killed—may have forgotten how little respect his own imposing physical presence commanded when anyone with a gun could kill.

PART III

1. In his study of the narratives of persisting offenders and desisting ex-offenders, Shadd Maruna (2001) uses results from the Liverpool Desistance Study, a "systematic comparison between the self-narratives of desisting [adult] ex-offenders and those of a carefully matched sample of active [adult] offenders" (38) living in Liverpool, England. In contrast to the theory that guilt and penance are necessary for reform, he finds that "although desisting interviewees do admit that many of the things they had done in the past were 'stupid mistakes,' they frequently blame this behavior on circumstances, their social situation, and other factors such as addiction and delinquent friends" (9).

2. For an in-depth discussion of some young women's "masculinity," see C. J. Pascoe's discussion of the "Basketball Girls" and the "Gay/Straight Alliance Girls" in her *Dude, You're a Fag* (2007).

3. In a world in which masculinity is associated with power and respect, it is unsurprising that women acting like men are granted more legitimacy than men acting like women (see Brown 2003: 46).

4. See Mimi Schippers's discussion (2002) of "gender maneuvering."

5. See also Patricia Gagne and Richard Tewksbury's discussion (1998) of transsexual men and the ways in which they simultaneously resist and reproduce gender norms: "They accepted the [gender] binary system; it was only their original placement within the binary that disturbed and dismayed most respondents" (98).

CHAPTER 5

1. For interesting discussions of the importance of outsiders for challenging bureaucratic inertia and for generating innovative strategies in a labor-organizing context, see Voss and Sherman (2000) and Ganz (2000).

2. For interesting analyses of the relationship between partial repression and political resistance, see Loveman (1998) and Zhao (1998).

3. In his study of United Farm Workers organizing in the 1960s, Marshall Ganz (2000) writes that a group's capacity to make sense of and act effectively in its environment, what he calls its "strategic capacity," depends on the diversity of the repertoires and resources of which its leadership can make use. In the case of the farmworkers, a combination of young Latino workers, older white communist organizers, and young well-educated students were able to forge effective strategies together.

4. Maruna (2001: 12) found that "desisting ex-offenders emphasize the desire to make some important contribution to their communities, and in particular to individuals like themselves who find themselves in trouble with the law." According to Maruna, an estimated 72 percent of the professional counselors working in the more than ten thousand substance-abuse treatment centers in the United States are former substance abusers themselves (103).

CONCLUSION

1. For more about the Justice Reinvestment project of the Council of State Governments, see www.justicereinvestment.org.

BIBLIOGRAPHY

AFSC (American Friends Service Committee). 1971. *Struggle for Justice: A Report on Crime and Punishment in America.* New York: Hill and Wang.

Alonso, Alejandro A. 2004. "Racialized Identities and the Formation of Black Gangs in Los Angeles." *Urban Geography* 25:658–74.

Armstrong, Elizabeth. 2002. *Forging Gay Identities: Organizing Sexuality in San Francisco, 1950–1994.* Chicago: University of Chicago Press.

Beccaria, Cesare. 1764/1819. *Of Crimes and Punishments.* Philadelphia: Philip H. Nicklin.

Becker, Howard S. 1963. *Outsiders: Studies in the Sociology of Deviance.* Glencoe, IL: Free Press.

Benjamin, Jessica. 1988. *The Bonds of Love: Psychoanalysis, Feminism, and the Problem of Domination.* New York: Pantheon Books.

Bentham, Jeremy. 1811/1830. *The Rationale of Punishment.* London: Robert Heward.

Bourdieu, Pierre. 1977. *Outline of a Theory of Practice.* Cambridge: Oxford University Press.

———. 1990. *The Logic of Practice.* Cambridge: Polity Press.

———. 1997. *Pascalian Meditations.* Palo Alto, CA: Stanford University Press.

Breiman, Harris, and T. Pete Bonner. 2001. "Support Groups for Men in Prison: The Fellowship of the King of Hearts." In Don Sabo, Terry A. Kupers, and Willie London (eds.), *Prison Masculinities*. Philadelphia: Temple University Press.

Brown, Lyn Mikel. 2003. *Girlfighting: Betrayal and Rejection Among Girls*. New York: New York University Press.

Brown, Wendy. 1992. "Finding the Man in the State." *Feminist Studies* 18 (1): 7–34.

Burawoy, Michael. 1979. *Manufacturing Consent: Changes in the Labor Process under Monopoly Capitalism*. Chicago, IL: University of Chicago Press.

Burton-Rose, Daniel. 2001. "The Anti-Exploits of Men Against Sexism, 1977–78." In Don Sabo, Terry A. Kupers, and Willie London (eds.), *Prison Masculinities*. Philadelphia: Temple University Press.

Butler, Judith. 1993. *Bodies That Matter: On the Discursive Limits of "Sex."* New York: Routledge.

Canada, Geoffrey. *Fist Stick Knife Gun: A Personal History of Violence in America*. Boston: Beacon Press.

Chodorow, Nancy. 1978. *The Reproduction of Mothering*. Berkeley: University of California Press.

Cloward, Richard, and Lloyd Ohlin. 1960. *Delinquency and Opportunity: A Theory of Delinquent Gangs*. Glencoe, IL: Free Press.

Cohen, John. 1991. "NOMAS: Challenging Male Supremacy." *Changing Men* (Winter/Spring): 45–46.

Connell, R. W. 1987. *Gender and Power: Society, the Person and Sexual Politics*. Sydney, Australia: Allen and Unwin.

———. 1995. *Masculinities*. Sydney, Australia: Allen and Unwin.

———. 2005. "Change Among the Gatekeepers: Men, Masculinities, and Gender Equality in the Global Arena." *Signs* 30 (3): 1801–24.

Connell, R. W., and James W. Messerschmidt. 2005. "Hegemonic Masculinity." *Gender and Society* 19 (6): 829–59.

Cooper, William. 1991. *Behold a Pale Horse*. Flagstaff, AZ: Light Technology Publications.

Delpit, Lisa. 1995. *Other People's Children: Cultural Conflict in the Class-room*. New York: New Press.

Denborough, David. 2001. "Grappling with Issues of Privilege: A Male Prison Worker's Perspective." In Don Sabo, Terry A. Kupers, and Willie London (eds.), *Prison Masculinities*. Philadelphia: Temple University Press.

Fanon, Frantz. 1963. *The Wretched of the Earth*. New York: Grove Press.

Feeley, Malcolm, and Jonathan Simon. 1992. "The New Penology: Notes on the Emerging Strategy of Corrections and Its Implications." *Criminology* 30 (4): 449–74.

Foucault, Michel. 1977. *Discipline and Punish: The Birth of the Prison*. New York: Vintage Books.

Freeman, Jo. 1972–73. "The Tyranny of Structurelessness." *Berkeley Journal of Sociology* 17:151–65.

Freud, Sigmund. 1930/1961. *Civilization and Its Discontents*. New York: W. W. Norton and Company.

Gagne, Patricia, and Richard Tewksbury. 1998. "Conformity Pressures and Gender Resistance among Transgendered Individuals." *Social Problems* 45 (1): 81–101.

Ganz, Marshall. 2000. "Resources and Resourcefulness: Leadership, Strategy and Organization in the Unionization of California Agriculture (1959–1966)." *American Journal of Sociology* 105: 1003–62.

Garland, David. 2001. *The Culture of Control: Crime and Social Order in Contemporary Society*. Chicago: University of Chicago Press.

Goffman, Erving. 1961. *Asylums: Essays on the Social Situation of Mental Patients*. Garden City, NY: Doubleday.

Gouldner, Alvin. 1973. "The Sociologist as Partisan." In *For Sociology*. London: Allen Lane.

Haraszti, Miklos. 1978. *A Worker in a Worker's State*. New York: Universe Books.

Hearn, Jeff. 1998. *The Violences of Men*. London: Sage Publications.

Hochschild, Arlie R. 1983. *The Managed Heart: Commercialization of Human Feeling*. Berkeley: University of California Press.

Hood-Williams, John. 2001. "Gender, Masculinities and Crime: From Structures to Psyches." *Theoretical Criminology* 5:37–60.

Jankowski, Martin Sanchez. 1991. *Islands in the Street: Gangs and American Urban Society*. Berkeley: University of California Press.

Keiser, R.L. 1969. *The Vice Lords: Warriors of the Streets*. New York: Holt, Rinehart and Winston.

Kennedy, Randall L. 1999/2000. "Who Can Say 'Nigger'? ... And Other Considerations." *Journal of Blacks in Higher Education* 26:86–96.

Klubock, Thomas Miller. 1996. "Working-Class Masculinity, Middle-Class Morality and Labor Politics in the Chilean Copper Mines." *Journal of Social History* 30 (2): 435–63.

Lever, Janet. 1976. "Sex Differences in the Games Children Play." *Social Problems* 23:478–87.

Levitt, Steven D., and Sudhier Alladi Venkatesh. 2000. "An Economic Analysis of a Drug-Selling Gang's Finances." *Quarterly Journal of Economics* 115 (3) 755–89.

Little, Sara S., and John Abbate. 1996. *A Study of Recidivism Rates of Youth in Minimum Security*. Cranston: Rhode Island Training School.

Lombroso, Cesare. 1911. *Criminal Man*. New York: Putnam.

Lorber, Judith. 2005. *Breaking the Bowls: Degendering and Feminist Change*. New York: W.W. Norton and Company.

Loveman, Mara. 1998. "High-Risk Collective Action: Defending Human Rights in Chile, Uruguay, and Argentina." *American Journal of Sociology* 104:477–525.

Lynch, Mona. 2000. "Rehabilitation as Rhetoric: The Ideal of Reformation in Contemporary Parole Discourse and Practices." *Punishment and Society* 2:40–65.

Majors, R., and J.M. Billson. 1992. *Cool Pose: The Dilemmas of Black Manhood in America*. New York: Lexington Books.

Marcuse, Herbert. 1955. *Eros and Civilization*. Boston: Beacon Press.

Martinson, Robert. 1974. "What Works—Questions and Answers about Prison Reform." *The Public Interest* 35:22–54.

Maruna, Shadd. 2001. *Making Good: How Ex-Offenders Reform and Rebuild Their Lives*. Washington DC: American Psychological Association.

Matza, David. 1964. *Delinquency and Drift*. New York: Wiley.

McAdam, Doug. 1982. *Political Process and the Development of Black Insurgency, 1930–1970*. Chicago: University of Chicago Press.

Mead, George Herbert. 1934. *Mind, Self and Society*. Chicago: University of Chicago Press.

Merton, Robert. 1968. *Social Theory and Social Structure*. New York: Free Press.

Messerschmidt, James W. 1986. *Capitalism, Patriarchy, and Crime: Toward a Socialist Feminist Criminology*. Totowa, NJ: Rowman and Littlefield.

———. 1993. *Masculinities and Crime: Critique and Reconceptualization of Theory*. New York: Rowman and Littlefield.

———. 1997. *Crime as Structured Action: Gender, Race, Class, and Crime in the Making*. Thousand Oaks, CA: Sage Publications.

———. 2000. *Nine Lives: Adolescent Masculinities, the Body, and Violence*. New York: Westview Press.

———. 2004. *Flesh and Blood: Adolescent Gender Diversity and Violence*. New York: Rowman and Littlefield.

Messner, Michael A. 1992. *Power at Play: Sports and the Problem of Masculinity*. Boston: Beacon Press.

Meyer, John W., and Brian Rowan. 1977. "Institutionalized Organizations: Formal Structure as Myth and Ceremony." *American Journal of Sociology* 83:340–63.

Pascoe, C.J. 2007. *Dude, You're a Fag: Masculinity and Sexuality in High School*. Berkeley: University of California Press.

Payne, Charles M. 1995. *I've Got the Light of Freedom: The Organizing Tradition and the Mississippi Freedom Struggle*. Berkeley: University of California Press.

Peacock, Dean. 2003. "Building on a Legacy of Social Justice Activism: Enlisting Men as Gender Justice Activists in South Africa." *Men and Masculinities* 5 (3): 325–28.

Pfeffer, Jeffrey. 1981. *Power in Organizations*. Marshfield, MA: Pitman Publishing.

Pfeffer, Jeffrey, and Gerald Salancik. 1978. *The External Control of Organizations: A Resource Dependence Perspective*. New York: Harper and Row.

Piven, Frances Fox, and Richard Cloward. 1977. *Poor People's Movements*. New York: Pantheon Books.

Platt, Anthony M. 1969. *The Child-Savers: The Invention of Delinquency*. Chicago: University of Chicago Press.

Quetelet, Adolphe. 1833. *The Propensity to Crime*. Brussels: Hayez.

Rothman, David. 1971. *The Discovery of the Asylum*. Boston: Little Brown.

Rusche, Georg, and Otto Kirchheimer. 1939. *Punishment and Social Structure*. New York: Columbia University Press.

Schippers, Mimi. 2002. *Rockin' Out of the Box: Gender Maneuvering in Alternative Hard Rock*. New Jersey: Rutgers University Press.

Scull, Andrew T. 1977. *Decarceration: Community Treatment and the Deviant—A Radical View*. Englewood Cliffs, NJ: Prentice-Hall Inc.

Sewell, Tony. 1997. *Black Masculinities and Schooling: How Black Boys Survive Modern Schooling*. Stoke on Trent, UK: Trentham Books.

Simon, Jonathan. 1993. *Poor Discipline: Parole and the Social Control of the Underclass, 1890–1990*. Chicago: University of Chicago.

Sitkin, S. 1992. "Learning through Failure: The Strategy of Small Losses." In B. M. Staw and L. L. Cummings (eds.), *Research in Organizational Behavior*, vol. 14.Greenwich, CT: JAI Press.

Staples, Robert. 1982. *Black Masculinity: The Black Male's Role in American Society*. San Francisco: Black Scholars Press.

Sykes, Gresham M. 1958. *The Society of Captives*. Princeton, NJ: Princeton University Press.

Texas Youth Commission. 2002. *Resocialization Participant Manual*. Austin: Texas Youth Commission.

Thorne, Barrie. 1993. *Gender Play: Girls and Boys in School*. New Brunswick, NJ: Rutgers University Press.

Tomsen, Stephen. 2006. "Homophobic Violence, Cultural Essentialism and Shifting Sexual Identities." *Social Legal Studies* 15:389.

Voss, Kim, and Rachel Sherman. 2000. "Breaking the Iron Law of
Oligarchy: Union Revitalization in the American Labor Movement." *American Journal of Sociology* 106:303–49.

Wacquant, Loic. 2001. "Deadly Symbiosis: When Ghetto and Prison
Meet and Mesh." *Punishment and Society* 3 (1): 95–133.

West, Candace, and Don H. Zimmerman. 1991. "Doing Gender." In
J. Lorber and S.A. Farrell (eds.), *The Social Construction of Gender.*
Newbury Park, CA: Sage Publications.

Willis, Paul. 1977. *Learning to Labor.* New York: Columbia University
Press.

Wilson, James Q. 1983. *Thinking About Crime.* New York: Basic Books.
———. 1989. *Bureaucracy: What Government Agencies Do and Why:* Basic
Books.

Young, Jock. 1999. *The Exclusive Society.* London: Sage Publications.

Zhao, Dingxin. 1998. "Ecologies of Social Movements: Student Mobi-
lization During the 1989 Pro-democracy Movement in Beijing."
American Journal of Sociology 103 (6): 1493–529.

INDEX

Text:	10/15 Janson
Display:	Janson
Compositor:	Toppan Best-set Premedia Limited
Indexer:	Thérèse Shere
Printer and binder:	Maple-Vail Manufacturing Group